THE WOMAN AT THE WELL

THE WOMAN AT THE WELL

By

ADRIAN VAN KAAM, C.S.Sp.

EPIPHANY ASSOCIATION
947 Tropical Avenue
Pittsburgh, PA 15216-3031

Imprimi Potest: *Rev. Philip J. Haggerty, C.C.Sp.*
Provincial

Nihil Obstat: *Rev. William J. Winter, S.T.D.*
Censor Librorum

Imprimatur: *Most Rev. Vincent M. Leonard, D.D.*
Bishop of Pittsburgh

December 2nd, 1976

This book is dedicated
to Bert van Croonenburg
with gratitude and affection

ISBN 1-880982-03-X

TABLE OF CONTENTS

BOOKS BY THE AUTHOR

The Art of Existential Counseling
Become Jesus: The Diary of a Soul Touched by God (co-editor)
The Commandments: Ten Ways to a Happy Life
and a Healthy Soul (co-author)
Commitment: Key to Christian Maturity (co-author)
Commitment: A Workbook and Study Guide (co-author)
Divine Guidance (co-author)
The Dynamics of Spiritual Self Direction
Foundations for Personality Study
Harnessing Stress (co-author)
Healthy and Holy Under Stress (co-author)
Looking for Jesus
The Music of Eternity
On Being Involved
On Being Yourself
The Participant Self (co-author)
Personality Fulfillment in the Spiritual Life
The Power of Appreciation (co-author)
Practicing the Prayer of Presence (co-author)
Religion and Personality
Religious Presence of the Christian
The Roots of Christian Joy
Songs for Every Season (co-author)
Spirituality and the Gentle Life
Stress and the Search for Happiness (co-author)
The Tender Farewell of Jesus
The Transcendent Self
The Vowed Life
The Woman at the Well
Woman's Guide to the Catechism of the Catholic Church (co-author)

Formative Spirituality Series:

Fundamental Formation, Vol. I
Human Formation, Vol. II
Formation of the Human Heart, Vol. III
Scientific Formation, Vol. IV
Traditional Formation, Vol. V
Transcendent Formation, Vol. VI
Transcendence Therapy, Vol. VII

FOREWORD

The Gospel of St. John lends itself well to a meditative reading that may transform us inwardly. St. John, communicating his experience of God, enlightens his readers about their inner pilgrimage. His words move us toward a fuller share in the life that Jesus came to give us. Even if it would be true that the original text of this Gospel has been rewritten by later editors, it is also true that the Church accepted these writings in their final form as a faithful expression of her own thought and feeling; it gave this text the mark of divine revelation, of the Spirit's infallible speaking to all of the faithful.

This Gospel is meaningful for our inner formation because it presents a coherent Christian spirituality that is striking and personal; it is written in a dwelling style more cyclic and meditatively repetitive than linear and logical.

The narrative of Jesus' meeting with the woman at the well is in a sense an echo of the whole of St. John's Gospel, for this touching story mirrors in vivid miniature the keypoints of its spiritual doctrine. The darkness the woman finds herself in, her hidden longing for liberation and fulfillment, the living water he invites her to, the coming of the true light into her life, worship in spirit and in truth, going out to other people in love — all these matters are spoken about elsewhere in this Gospel. Already in the prologue these themes are at least implicitly present. We find them also in the narrative of the nightly visit of Nicodemus, in the last discourse of Jesus and in many other places. This Gospel speaks time and again about that divine invitation given to all of us to leave the darkness of sinful attachments and enter his light. If we accept his invitation, he assures us that we will meet the Father in Jesus, that we, like the woman at the well, will receive the water that alone can quench our thirst.

God for St. John is the light that shines through the darkness of our alienation. Incarnation means for him that the divine light comes into the world to dispel our darkness, bringing new graced life. Every human creature is gently invited, as was the Samaritan woman, to drink of living waters with the promise that they will well up within him to everlasting life.

The life promised to the woman is the transcendent inner life of God himself. He raises us lovingly far beyond our innate human possibilities; he pulls us toward an ever deeper intimacy with him. He makes us share in his own outpouring of divine love for all people and all creation. This explains why the person touched by this light experiences a new love and care for people. The conversion of the Samaritan woman ends with her going forth from Jesus to bring the good tidings to people in Sychar. Earlier Jesus himself had given up his well deserved rest and recollection in solitude by the well so that he could be of help to this woman. Later when the disciples return with food he declines to eat, concerned as he is with the salvation of the Samaritans who approach him. This manifestation of love for others as an expression of love for God is a reverberation of the message of both the Gospel and the letters of St. John.

John's message is thus briefly this: every person born in this world finds himself in darkness. He longs for light, for the fullness of truth, love and life. This fullness finds its source in the Father who *is* truth, love and life. But the Father cannot be met, touched, heard directly. He can be met, however, and experienced in his Incarnate Word, who came into the world to dispel the darkness in which people dwell. Little by little in a loving presence to Jesus the human thirst for infinite love and light will be quenched, fully in the eschaton, but beginning already here on earth. "Whoever believes in me believes not in me but in the one who sent me, and whoever sees me, sees the one who sent me. I, the light, have come into the world, so that whoever believes in me need not stay in the dark anymore" (Jn. 12:44-46).

Jesus is thus the divinity of the Father present; and yet St. John wants to make clear that he is truly one of us, really human except for sin. He did not keep aloof from our human situation. This concern of the Evangelist is mirrored in his narrative of Jesus' meeting with the woman: his being tired and thirsty as any other human being would be after a long and exhausting trip; his asking for a drink of water; his kind and caring talk with the woman; his human eye for fields, grain, harvest; his vivid imagination playing with these earthly appearances as symbols for his thoughts; his wonder and joy about the cordial reception given him by the Samaritans. This story echoes the same human touch we find elsewhere in this Gospel: Jesus' warm friendship with John himself, with the disciples, with Mary, Martha and their brother Lazarus.

All of this divine and human love is not only offered to the woman at the well but through the Holy Spirit to each of us: "On the last day and greatest day of the festival, Jesus stood there and cried out: 'If any man is thirsty, let him come to me! Let the man come and drink who believes in me! As scripture says: From his breast shall flow fountains of living water. He was speaking of the Spirit which those who believed in him were to receive; for there was no Spirit as yet because Jesus had not yet been glorified' " (Jn. 7:37-39).

A meditative reading of the following pages, may, it is hoped, reawaken us to the living water flowing to each of us from the interiority of Jesus.

ACKNOWLEDGMENTS

I am very grateful to my colleagues at the Institute of Man, Bert van Croonenburg, C.S.Sp., S.T.D., and Susan Annette Muto, Ph.D., both of whom offered me many helpful criticisms and suggestions. I thank Sister Margaret Gall, S.D.R., for her generous typing and proofreading of the manuscript and Sister Dorothy Majewski for her kind assistance in proof reading and the many other secretarial chores that accompany the preparation of a publication.

THE WOMAN AT THE WELL: AN OVERVIEW

When Jesus heard that the Pharisees had found out that he was making and baptizing more disciples than John—"though in fact it was his disciples who baptized, not Jesus himself—' he left Judaea and went back to Galilee. This meant that he had to cross Samaria.

On the way he came to the Samaritan town called Sychar, near the land that Jacob gave to his son Joseph. Jacob's well is there and Jesus, tired by the journey, sat straight down by the well. It was about the sixth hour. When a Samaritan woman came to draw water, Jesus said to her, "Give me a drink." His disciples had gone into the town to buy food. The Samaritan Woman said to him, "What? You are a Jew and you ask me, a Samaritan, for a drink?"—Jews, in fact, do not associate with Samaritans. Jesus replied:

> If you only knew what God is offering
> and who it is that is saying to you:
> Give me a drink,
> you would have been the one to ask,
> and he would have given you living water.

"You have no bucket, sir," she answered, "and the well is deep: how could you get this living water? Are you a greater man than our father Jacob who gave us this well and drank from it himself with his sons and his cattle?" Jesus replied:

Whoever drinks this water
will get thirsty again;
but anyone who drinks the water that I shall give
will never be thirsty again:
the water that I shall give
will turn into a spring inside him, welling up to eternal life.

"Sir," said the woman, "give me some of that water, so that I may never get thirsty and never have to come here again to draw water." "Go and call your husband," said Jesus to her, "and come back here." The woman answered, "I have no husband." He said to her, "You are right to say, 'I have no husband'; for although you have had five, the one you have now is not your husband. You spoke the truth there." "I see you are a prophet, sir," said the woman. "Our fathers worshiped on this mountain, while you say that Jerusalem is the place where one ought to worship," Jesus said:

Believe me, woman, the hour is coming
when you will worship the Father
neither on this mountain nor in Jerusalem.
You worship what you do not know;
we worship what we do know;
for salvation comes from the Jews.
But the hour will come—in fact it is here already—

when true worshipers will worship the Father in spirit and
truth:
that is the kind of worshiper
the Father wants.
God is spirit,
and those who worship
must worship in spirit and truth.

The woman said to him, "I know that Messiah—
that is, Christ—is coming; and when he comes he will
tell us everything." "I who am speaking to you," said
Jesus, "I am he."

At this point his disciples returned, and were
surprised to find him speaking to a woman, though
none of them asked, "What do you want from her?"
or, "Why are you talking to her?" The woman put
down her water jar and hurried back to the town to tell
the people, "Come and see a man who has told me
everything I ever did; I wonder if he is the Christ?"
This brought people out of the town and they started
walking toward him.

Meanwhile, the disciples were urging him, "Rabbi,
do have something to eat"; but he said, "I have food
to eat that you do not know about." So the disciples
asked one another, "Has someone been bringing him
food?" But Jesus said:

My food
is to do the will of the one who sent me,
and to complete his work.
Have you not got a saying:
Four months and then the harvest?
Well, I tell you:

Look around you, look at the fields;
already they are white, ready for harvest!
Already the reaper is being paid his wages,
already he is bringing in the grain for eternal life,
and thus sower and reaper rejoice together.
For here the proverb holds good:
one sows, another reaps;
I sent you to reap
a harvest you had not worked for.
Others worked for it;
and you have come into the rewards of their trouble.

Many Samaritans of that town had believed in him on the strength of the woman's testimony when he said, "He told me all I have ever done," so, when the Samaritans came up to him, they begged him to stay with them. He stayed for two days, and when he spoke to them many more came to believe; and they said to the woman, "Now we no longer believe because of what you told us; we have heard him ourselves and we know that he really is the savior of the world" (Jn. 4:1-42).

We presented this text in its entirety because we should begin our prayerful reading with an overview of the chapter we have chosen to reflect upon before the Lord. Such an overview gives us an initial feeling for the story as a whole. Afterwards we may devoutly dwell as long as we want on any detail; each word may evoke holy sentiments, prolonged reflection and personal meditation. At such moments we may forget how the details that inspire us fit into the overall passage. However, by recalling our earlier reading of the whole chapter—as we are doing now—we will be able to link each sentence with the basic meaning of the story.

This Gospel narrative begins by telling us that Jesus travelled from Judea to Galilee. Our Lord wanted to leave Judea because he had been told that the Pharisees had become anxious about the rumors that he had been baptizing even more people than John himself. They felt uneasy about his growing popularity. Their mounting concern could have led to his arrest. Jesus wanted to avoid captivity and death before the hour appointed by his Father. He therefore withdrew from Judea to Galilee. Throughout the Gospel Judea is a place where Jesus finds opposition, where he is not made to feel welcome.

The shortest way to Galilee would take him through the lands of the Samaritans. Jews looked down on Samaritans as people unfaithful to the covenant and the prophets. After the Assyrian captivity a Jewish and pagan population was left in Samaria. The Samaritans Jesus will meet there were the descendants of this mixed population. They had drifted away from Jewish faith and worship. They still revered Moses and the Mosaic Torah but did not hold to many other views of the chosen people. They also refused to center their worship with the Jews in the temple of Jerusalem. The latter rejected them angrily as half pagans; whenever they chanced to meet one another the air was filled with hostility and suspicion.

The crossing through Samaria seemed to have no other reason than that it was the shortest way to Galilee. Yet the Spirit inspires him to ministry in Samaria by speaking to him in a travel situation in which the will of the Father reveals itself. So it came about that Jesus, during his trip to Galilee to escape possible arrest in Judea, met with a Samaritan woman and stayed two days in a Samaritan village where he became acknowledged by many as the savior of the world.

The Samaritan woman represents not only a typical Samaritan but the average human person. In her talk with Jesus she shows that she, like most people, is preoccupied with the relief of daily needs so that life may go on smoothly. One of her needs is to obtain drinking water with the least possible expenditure of time and energy. Her spiritual life is clearly not her great concern.

In his travel from Judea through Samaria, Jesus along with his disciples reached the village of Sychar, located in this territory. Tired and thirsty he sat down by a well which was called Jacob's well because the patriarch Jacob, his people and cattle, used to drink from it. The Lord had sent the disciples to Sychar itself to buy some food for them. A Samaritan woman, who probably had a bad reputation because of her loose life, came for water. He attempts a conversation with her, but she makes him feel immediately the barrier between Jews and Samaritans. She sees Jesus initially as a Jew who should not want to associate with her or any other Samaritan. In the beginning of their conversation, she consistently misunderstands Jesus and challenges everything he is saying. He answers her challenges in his own way. It is this interplay between her challenges and his answers that keeps the talk alive and progressing.

Jesus opens the conversation by asking her for a drink. She voices somewhat unkindly her surprise about a Jew asking a Samaritan for a drink. He tells her that she does not realize who is asking her, that he himself could give her living water which would be a lasting source of life. The woman assumes that Jesus is speaking about some kind of natural water. Even when Jesus explains to her that the water he speaks about will quench her thirst for ever, she imagines that he must be talking about a magical supply of ordinary water. She has no clue as yet that he is talking about grace, about himself as gift to man. She persists in asking for a miracle: running water for her home.

Then, suddenly, Jesus penetrates her preoccupation with household matters by asking her to call her husband. This request succeeds in shifting her attention from housekeeping and running water to her own unhappy life and her vain search for a solution in various liaisons. She no longer tries to escape from herself; she lets her defenses down and allows herself to be engaged in a conversation about the things that really matter in human life. She confesses that she has no husband. Now, being in the truth, she is able to hear Jesus' revelation about her own sinful life. She sees him as a prophet. Yet she still tries to change the subject, to sidetrack the Lord by bringing up an issue not intimately bound to her private problems: she asks his judgment in the age-long dispute between Jew and Samaritan about where to worship God—in Jerusalem or Mount Gerizim? Jesus tells her that this question is no longer relevant. He refers to the fact that after his death it will be the dynamic movement of the Spirit in all mankind that will lead everywhere to true worship of the Father in Jesus.

Jesus speaks to her about worshiping in spirit and in truth. Truth here is not simply the opposite of intellectual falsehood or misunderstanding. Rather it means living as a whole person in the Light of God's presence as opposed to dwelling in the darkness of sin. To worship in truth means to encounter as a total human person the Presence of the Father in Jesus, a personal encounter with God. To be a worshiper in truth is to be caught up into a personal intimate presence to God in Jesus and to live out of this presence. It is that truth which sets us free. This transforming presence is the work of the Spirit. Therefore two ideas are here joined together: worship in spirit and in truth.

Jesus now tells her that he is the Messiah. Touched by his grace and his presence, she opens up to him in faith and hastens away to bring the good tidings to other Samaritans. This demonstrates concretely how worship in spirit and in truth will become possible for all men and not only for one race, class or sex.

In the meantime the disciples had returned with the food bought in Sychar and urge him to eat. Jesus tries to make clear to them that he does not feel like eating at this moment, overcome as he is by an inner nourishment which is for him doing the Father's will and completing the work he has sent him to do. They are mystified and Jesus uses the occasion to explain about his mission, a mission which will be shared by his followers. He teaches them that the word of God may bear fruit immediately as it did in the case of this Samaritan woman. In this instance there is no interval between the sowing and the reaping. He makes clear also that it will not always be that way. Some have to be sowers who will not see the fruit of their labors; others will be reapers like Jesus at this moment. He tells them that the fields are already ripe, white for the harvest; he refers here to the coming of the Samaritans in their white garments, who are already moving towards him. He adds that both sowers and reapers will some day together enjoy the harvest, which rejoicing will be their reward.

The story ends in a harvest of Samaritan believers. Many Samaritans of Sychar, after listening to the woman's story, "come and see" for themselves the Jewish stranger about whom she had told them. They invite him to stay with them. He does so for two days. During that stay many more come to believe in him. Their faith is based on a personal experience of Jesus. They see him not as the king and liberator of Israel but as the savior of all men and women, of Jews, Samaritans and Gentiles. They acknowledge him as the *savior of the world.*

The end of the story suggests two stages in our

coming to faith. First, the witness of another evokes a certain openness to the possibility of faith. Then hearing Jesus' word, encountering him personally, being touched by his grace leads to the living faith that Jesus is the savior.

The self revelation of Jesus in this story is gradual and striking; so is the growth of faith in the woman and the other Samaritans. She sees in the man at the well first a Jew, next a prophet, then the Messiah, and finally, with other Samaritans, the savior of the world.

GIVE ME A DRINK

" . . . *he [Jesus] had to cross Samaria. On the way he came to the Samaritan town called Sychar . . . Jacob's well is there and Jesus, tired by the journey, sat straight down by the well"* (Jn. 4:1-42).

Fatigued from his travel, Jesus had to rest by a watering place; he reveals himself as one of us, vulnerable, with a fragile body, with a mind that tires. The endless walk across the land, the dusty road, the burning of the sun, the chatter of followers had taken much out of him. At last a spring: to be left in peace, to sit down without worry, to taste the water of the earth freshly bubbling up in the well whose stone wall he felt pressing against his weary back. He felt hungry. He had sent his disciples off to get some food. At last, alone with his aching body, his weary feet, alone also with his Father in Heaven. Alone but not for long.

" . . . *a Samaritan woman came to draw water . . .* "

He sees her coming, hand high on the water jug perched on her head. He realizes his solitude will be broken now for the sake of his Father's will, for the consolation of a soul in sadness, for countless others who will find comfort in this story of divine compassion.

Slightly bored, the woman makes her daily round to the well. She notices a weary traveller sitting there dressed like a Jew. He surely will not talk to her. He will pretend not even to see her. Jews avoid Samaritans like one avoids a dreadful disease.

How little she suspects what is going to happen. A few moments and this trip to the spring will be an immortal event to be recounted by people of many tongues, cultures and generations. She had come to draw water; instead she will draw the attention of the Eternal and of countless people all over the earth. She could not guess the role a little woman at a well was called to play in the pattern of Providence.

A passionate woman, craving for sympathy, an unconventional lady but not self-righteous as a Pharisee, pedantic as a Scribe, cunning as a Priest. Outspoken and spontaneous, she had kept alive the spark of hope in her saddened soul. Vexed by disappointment, the collapse of many marriages, bewildered by confused desires, she hungers for meaning in her humdrum life.

Casually she approaches the fountain, unaware that she among thousands has been chosen to meet in person the Eternal, to feel the touch of an infinite tenderness. The maker of the universe hides in the tired frame propped up against the wall of the well. She does not know him.

Each of us may drift through life casually like this lonely Samaritan. For each of us, our meeting with the Eternal may happen at a moment least expected. Like a flash, Jesus may light up the depth of our soul. He may appear to us under the veil of the least of his brothers and sisters suffering along the road. Who knows the day or the hour that Jesus may reach out to him?

We are engrossed in anxiously guarding our water jar as if it were the globe itself. We run around drawing water from countless wells; the water of praise to refresh our failing self-esteem, the water of success to keep alive a sense of importance, the water of pleasure to delight our senses. Poor Samaritans that we are. Meanwhile the Eternal may be waiting around the corner with living water to nourish our deepest self. He may be waiting at a curve of the busy road along which our life is hastily speeding to its end.

Stumbling around in a murky night of small commitments, petty worries, little lusts and useless irritations we forget that Jesus may come like a thief in the night. He did so in the night of the Samaritan woman. She was on the brink of spiritual starvation. She wanted abundant life and had sought for it in many liaisons. He came to tell her that life cannot be abundant without him as the living water. It is only Jesus who brings joy to our life. She could truly repeat for the rest of her days, "When he came there was no light; when he was gone there was no darkness."

Jesus' presence gives majesty to the meanest of people. This happens when they listen to his word. The voice of man must be still that he may hear the voice of Jesus.

"Jesus said to her, 'Give me a drink' ".

He knows the checkered life of this woman, how high she will have to rise to enter into the life of the spirit. A first step upwards is a deed of generosity—to go out of herself, to make a little crack in the prison of self-absorption, no longer to hide in her shell, to open it a little like the shell fish does, to let the wide nourishing sea of eternity flow into a dried up, sheltered life.

Spiritual life means going beyond ourselves. Any going beyond, no matter how small is already a facilitating condition for that surpassing of ourselves toward an Infinite Love that beckons us, a love that Jesus calls our Father.

It would be presumptuous to try to go beyond ourselves too suddenly. We must humbly and in a relaxed way start from where we are. Jesus asked the woman for a small generous deed that makes sense in the midst of her workaday life: "Give me a drink." It is not important if during their further chat the water will be given or not. What counts is that he invites her to do what she can easily do for him here and now. What is crucial is that she allows herself to open up to his request, to go beyond herself and her little plans, that she creates in her soul space for generosity. For this will mean that she escapes the closed circle of interests that confine her within the case of her own little world, that she goes a little beyond herself and therewith a bit further on the road toward the Eternal Beyond.

If she can grant him wholeheartedly the tangible gift of water, she may be ready to grant him the intangible gift of the self she is. But then she must give without a shadow of selfish gain. Her togetherness with Jesus must be illumined by the light of a true gift. Not that a drink of water is of such worth by itself alone. What is worthwhile is a tangible expression of kindness and compassion toward a tired stranger.

Generosity plays a dynamic role in the life story of my opening up to Christ as he speaks to me in suffering people. "What you have done to the least of my brethren you have done to me." I must do what he asks us for his sake and not begrudge my generosity. Giving must not be a strategy to entice the other to respond likewise. Selfish giving sets free neither myself nor the other. It lures him into a subtle web of obligations. If he does not own up to them, he feels trapped. The more I grant him in a calculated way, the more he becomes the embarrassed inmate of my big-heartedness.

In needy friends, neighbors and adversaries, Jesus is asking me to give him a drink. He wants me to be generous so that I may be rescued from myself. Selfish giving makes me more of a shut-in in my own world. Calculated gentleness spins a subtle web around my life. I sound and look so good that I begin falsely to believe that I am that good. I may even be tempted to a life of spectacular generosity, especially in times when generosity is popular and gains me praise. Yet I am only buttressing the bars of my cage. Jesus is still asking, "Give me a drink." In spite of all my pretense I never relieve his thirst; I am still seeking myself, not him in those to whom I give.

In countless ways I can spoil the water I give others to drink. I may let them painfully feel their dependence upon me. My generosity may usurp their freedom. A gift with strings attached is not the gift Jesus is asking for when he begs of me a drink in those who are needy in spirit, wisdom and beauty, in learning, companionship or material necessities. I may play the game of sympathy and concern only to gain sympathy in return. Again this is not the drink Jesus is asking for.

Or I may be generous only to compel others to agree with my thoughts, feelings and projects, to bind them to me. By giving in this way I destroy the most precious gift Jesus wants me to grant to each of his brothers and sisters: the gift of freedom allowing each one of them to be and become who he is uniquely called to be in him, the Eternal Word.

Sometimes my gift may simply be the gift of a loving silence, the silence of listening fully to the secret of the self the other needs to reveal to me.

True generosity sets me free. To maintain this freedom in giving, I must respect my own limits as Jesus respected the limits of the Samaritan woman. He asked her simply to take time to give him a drink of water. He asked her what she could reasonably and calmly do at that moment of her life and that day. I should be as gentle with myself as Jesus was with the woman.

To foster a relaxed and wise generosity in my life, I should first of all be attentive to that kind of thirst of Jesus in my fellow men that I can relieve best because of the person I am. A parent should try first of all to ease the needs of spouse and children, a teacher of his pupils. An artist should sense the thirst of Jesus in the people that are aesthetically undernourished. The scientist should attempt to alleviate the need for knowledge in unfolding humanity. The therapist and counselor should answer the longing for emotional growth. The writer should relieve mankind's thirst for wisdom, beauty and inspiration. The graced humorist should bring the gift of laughter that people are hungry for. The farmer, carpenter, cook, plumber, mechanic, cab driver, life guard—all should hear the special thirst of mankind they are called to relieve. All should hear it as the voice of Jesus: "Give me a drink."

True giving reveals the spiritual person I may become in and through his grace. Giving is an event of the spirit, a first transcendence of my own captivity and the imprisoning I have imposed on others for my own selfish gains. Generosity shows my respect for my own transcendent uniqueness in Christ and my desire for the independent growth of others in his light.

Jesus himself may take over my petty generosity. He may begin to give, in and through me, to his Father and to his brothers and sisters in this world. I must allow him to radiate his divine generosity through my eyes, face and hands, my posture and motion. I must allow him to be present mysteriously in the tenderness of my touch, the mellowness of my voice, the gentle bend of my body. The generosity of Jesus in me symbolizes a fluent harmony of divine and human presence to those in need of me. Jesus in me makes them feel that they are lovable in spite of failings, acceptable in spite of the barriers they erected between themselves and the Divine.

The love of the Lord in us for the needy and the thirsty encourages them to bring into the light of the day their strengths and weaknesses, trusting that a compassionate Savior redeems them as they are. No greater gift can be given to people than the presence of persons who allow them to be themselves. No greater growth in the spirit can be experienced than that which divine acceptance makes possible.

Messenger of the Beyond,
Slow down this busy life
To taste the living waters
Flowing from your Spring of Love.
Open this shell a little with your wounded hand
That the ocean of eternity may rush into my dried up days.
Touch with tenderness the ruins of my life,
Light up the darkness of despair
That I no longer balance fearfully
My water jar as if it were the globe itself.
For you are waiting along the freeway
On which my days speed hastily to their end.
Life will collapse, the jar will be broken;
You alone remain the everlasting one in whom we share.
Your love gives majesty to the meanest people;
Create space in me that I may not begrudge
Nor spoil the generosity you called me to.
Free me from strategic giving
Luring people into indebtedness,
Making them inmates of my big-heartedness.
Radiate your love in friendly eyes,
In tenderness of touch, in mellowness of voice
That all may feel lovable in spite of countless failings.

GRACE AND RESISTANCE

"The Samaritan woman said to him, 'What? You are a Jew and You ask me, a Samaritan, for a drink?' Jews, in fact do not associate with Samaritans" (Jn. 4:9-10).

Jesus has humbly asked for a drink of water. The response of the woman is far from friendly. She sounds irritated, indignant, discourteous. All her life she has heard bad things about Jewish people. At times she had experienced their intolerance and responded in kind. Her heart was heavy with bitterness. She resented the haughty Jews who loathed her people and fiercely rejected them as heretics because they refused to abide by the revealed traditions and insisted on worshipping in their own Temple on Mount Gerizim instead of offering sacrifices in Jerusalem.

In her blunt response to the soft spoken appeal of this stranger, she refused to be polite; she refused even to call him "Sir," as she would do later. But the Lord of the Universe, rebuffed and humbled by one of his creatures, remains peaceful, poised and gentle. The radiant eyes in that drawn and haggard face keep looking at her with immense compassion. Graciously, he keeps speaking to her as if he had not heard her cutting remark. At the same time his divine interior speaks mysteriously to her interior, touching her with his grace and drawing her to himself.

Jesus does not directly answer the sour words of the woman. He does not tell her off nor does he say anything that could incense her. With the utmost consideration, he avoids gestures that may make her less open to the grace he is going to give her—the grace he so eagerly wants her to be receptive to.

There are times when we, like Jesus, must yield gently and withhold a justified defense, no matter how deeply we feel hurt. We should not become for others an occasion to become harsh and impervious to grace and love.

Jesus knew that the name of this lonely woman was written down in the loving design of his Father. It was the Father's will that she should open up to the Divine Light during this meeting with his Eternal Son. Our Lord, sitting by the well, is serenely faithful to what the Father wants him to say and do at this precious moment in the love story between God and a lonely woman. He knows that the Eternal Love delights in courting her in spite of her playing so hard to get. He is neither anxious nor overly concerned about her curt rejection of his friendly opening move. He knows that the Father's love for this woman is from eternity. He has carefully chosen the graces he will bestow on her at the appointed time.

If we are called to bring God's love to others, we should be available as relaxed cooperators with grace, as Jesus was. No undue haste, anxious ardor, subtle pressure or clever manipulation can hurry in the least the moment of grace for those who resist our best attempts. The rudeness of the woman cannot dampen the joy and gratefulness in Jesus that Divine Providence has brought her to him to receive life and light. He is faithful to what she is called to be.

. . . Jesus, my Lord, I too am often crude and resistant when you ask me for a drink of water. I too am caught in prejudice. I do not recognize your voice in so many who silently beg me for consideration, compassion, understanding. How often I pass them by, unfeelingly. Show yourself to me also in those I dislike, in those who differ from me. Teach me what I must do to please you in those who hurt me by discourtesy. Don't allow me to be an obstacle to your grace in others by refusing my sympathy and hardening their souls. . . .

How different the divine wisdom is from human wisdom. How gently Jesus foregoes any self-defense. How deep is his desire to draw a soul to himself, to unite her with himself by faith and divine love. Witness how eager he is to make her ready and receptive for these new tidings: that the burdens of the Old Testament are no longer necessary to become at one with the Lord of life. From now on, man will find repose in him by faith and love, by drinking from his living waters.

In spite of the woman's brusqueness, the tired man

by the well is filled with consolation; he is overwhelmed by a vision of how grace will flow from him like water from a living spring to inundate her and countless others the Father will draw to him, after he overcomes their anxious resistance, as he will now do with this woman. In gratitude, he offers his fatigue, the loss of his solitude, his weariness to the Father for the precious soul of this woman and of the many who will follow in her steps over the ages.

The resistance of the woman at the well merits our attention. It is an illustration of our own condition. It opens our eyes to secret plots against God's appeals to generosity. Her irritation makes us aware of the tactics employed by our own prejudices against our being gentle and giving. Her story is the tale of our excuses for not being compassionate with those who differ from us in background, temperament, ethnic, ethical or political persuasion. It is such prejudices that catch our life of compassion at the throat and choke off openness and love.

The case presented by the woman at the well is not an imaginary one. Alas, it is our own. Her resistance uncovers the core of the demonic system of resistance in each of us against being generous and gentle. This core is expounded in the curt reply she gave when the Lord humbly appealed to her to give him a drink of water, for he was the type of person she had learned to avoid. What is so poignant in this story is that human prejudice can be so blinding that it veils even the presence of God himself in the humblest of men.

We have built, alone or with others, a wall of

prejudices that prevents us from seeing God in those we secretly fear. We are unable to hear in them the silent voice of the Lord asking us for a drink of water. Our "divine radar", given to us by the Holy Spirit, has been turned off towards them. What turns it off is our fear. We fear them because of our insecurity, that deep insecurity that pervades all men since the fall. We can only overcome this anxiety if we learn to really trust our Father as Jesus did.

If we are secure in the Father's hands, we need not worry about the unkindness of aliens and strangers we meet in our life, about their refusal of our gift. Once we place ourselves and our good will in the hands of the Father, all our misgivings are abundantly met. What a peace-evoking thought: "My goodness and its consequences, even for those who resist me, rests lovingly in the hands of the Father." Can any thought be more assuring and uplifting than this? Lovingly and trustingly, we settle within his presence. As he fills us with his divine love and peace, every cell and atom of our person may be more permeated by his spirit of generosity. He may help us to rise each dawn with renewed courage to break through whatever prejudices may have accumulated in our life. Our spirit will be supported by his Spirit. Our willingness to give to those who are in need may grow more in harmony with him as we rest in his hands.

As the Father cares for the lonely sparrow, so he cares for us and through us for those who appeal to our love. If we see the fulfillment of our tasks as a gift to him, and through him to humanity, we can accomplish them with less resistance, with more harmony and ease. We may begin to abide in the faith that his love will help us not to stray beyond his care. Even if people disappoint our expectations, deride our gentleness, and despise our gift, we must rest assured that God allows all things to work together for our good. We must rejoice in the knowledge that the whole world is in his hands.

Wash away, O Living Waters, intolerance and indignation,
Dark specks disfiguring our life.
Let us no longer trudge through endless waste lands,
Our heart heavy with bitterness and dumb rejection
Of those who erode our expectations,
Our dreams of an early eschaton.
Make the appeal of thirsty strangers music to our ears;
Let us share with them the moisture left in the water jar
You placed upon our weary back when you sent us out
alone.
Keep us straight as an evergreen
When ravenous birds seek shelter in our branches.
Fill us with immense compassion
When arrogant people despise your gentleness
And deride your gift.
Hold our biting tongues, our furious gestures.
Let our incensed impatience not spoil the love story
Between the Eternal and the sinner who crosses our path.
Mitigate our anxious ardor, our spurious haste,
Our clever willfulness so eagerly outrunning your design.
Make us faithful to the holy destiny they do not yet suspect.
Let us nestle trustingly in your presence,
As in a cradle of peace, a hidden paradise.
Permeate every cell and atom of our being
With your spirit of generosity.
Fill us with the joy of knowing
That the whole world rests wholly in your hands.

GRACE AND RECEPTIVITY

"If you only knew what God is offering and who it is that is saying to you: Give me a drink, you would have been the one to ask, and we would have given you living water" (Jn. 4:10).

Jesus is not angry with the woman at the well. He wants her to be at home with him so that he may thaw the chill in her heart. Her answer had been unkind; her heart was not yet opened to what Jesus was giving and asking. He tries to help her see: *"If you only knew what God is offering,"* a gift that will mellow your mind, warm your heart, enlighten your spirit—a gift found in me alone. If you only knew who it is who asks you for a drink, you would give up your coolness and distance. You would sense that I am not after water, but after your soul. If you knew, then you would have been the one to ask me to let you drink from my fullness and I would have given you living water.

Our Lord asks her not merely for water but for her whole being. He wants to fill her with graces and give her to his Father as a new person filled with his own light and love.

The woman is still resisting. Her mind is tight and

small, crowded with misgivings and resentments. Her
heart is heavy with attachment to a loose and self-
centered life. She needs a wealth of graces to let the
light and strength of our Lord open up and widen her
heart. That is why our Lord said to her if you only
knew what God is offering and who it is that is saying
to you, give me a drink, you would give up your
defiance of my love, you would tune in to me, to my
silent inspiration, you would become still and
receptive.

The Lord speaks his *"If you only knew"* not only to
the woman at the well but to each of us. He speaks to
me:

> . . . *If you only knew that I am the incarnation of
> the Infinite Love you have been longing for deep in
> your heart. If you only knew that my longing for you
> surpasses infinitely your longing for me. If you only
> knew that I am burning with desire to fill you with the
> living water of grace and love, that my asking you
> anything is but a loving occasion for me to touch you,
> to make you into a new person. If you only knew that I
> cannot do so without your being receptive to me, then
> you would ask me to give you a drink of divine
> compassion and I would give you that living water. To
> really reach you, I need your asking. Without your
> receptivity I can do nothing, I am powerless in my love
> for you.*

To receive Jesus graciously is of greater import than
to give to him generously. Both are necessary. But

without Jesus we can do nothing; we cannot truly give anything, even to Him. And Jesus cannot make us givers when we do not receive him first. He has made his divine power dependent on our receptivity.

Life with Jesus is a story of receiving him and his Holy Spirit. Before we can give to others we must receive from the Spirit love and virtue, gentleness and strength, wisdom and pearls of insight. We grow in divine love by receiving these gifts daily. These gifts may come to us directly or through family, friends, culture, community. In turn we are asked by the Spirit to share our gifts with others in need of a drink of the waters of love and life.

Our gift of divine love and inspiration is never the gift of us alone. We give only from what we have received. At times we are called to be the dispenser, at times the recipient of his bounty.

Receiving is not simply a matter of seizing what Jesus offers us but of adoring what his gift symbolizes: Jesus himself.

There are ways of receiving which bear no trace of true receptivity. In greedy receiving we are so eager to enrich our spiritual life that we are preoccupied with what we can get and pay scant attention to the divine giver himself. Jesus' love is paralyzed when we are more interested in his presents than in his person.

We may fear to receive because we found that others tried to buy us by presents that were bribes. This fear may be so deeply rooted that it interferes even with our ability to receive graciously from the Lord. Inability to receive from the Lord and his people destroys the rhythm of giving and receiving on which growth in the life of the Spirit depends.

Receiving is a response to what lies beyond the gift. To receive graciously we should look more on the divine love of the heavenly giver than on the gift itself. Graciousness in receiving is also inspired by our awareness of Jesus' desire to find grateful persons to whom he can give what he bought for them with his blood.

To live a spiritual life is to excel in the art of receiving without fear or withholding. We should not fear for our freedom. Divine gifts are never meant to dominate us or diminish our freedom, to buy our love before we are willing to give it freely to him.

Open to Jesus in ourselves and others in receptivity and generosity, we live the divine dimension of giving and receiving. We take part in the love that illumines and warms a redeemed humanity, a love that asks only that we receive and give the countless blessings an eternal Presence bestows constantly on a disgruntled and anxious race.

We are invited, like the woman at the well, not only to receive but also to give and to receive in the very act of giving. God calls upon us in the demands of our fellow men. A simple appeal by a fellow human being is often veiled and mute. But it is in this veiled appeal that grace speaks to us without overwhelming us. The invitation of grace is often hidden, soft and gentle like the rains of spring, an invitation to play our part in the divine symphony. This invitation is at the same time the offering of a mysterious opportunity. We receive in the giving. It is the opportunity to grow in oneness with the Divine, source of light and goodness, to do penance for sin and imperfection by quiet generosity, to be a radiant pointer to the eschaton by lighting a little candle of compassion in the shadows of this world. It is an opportunity to be rescued from emptiness, to be filled with the Lord's own life of veneration of the Father and of compassion for the pained members of his body.

We must share in the compassion of our Lord not only for this woman, but for all who like her lost the horizon of the Divine in their plodding lives, who are bent over this earth and blind to heaven, who hear the sounds of daily chatter, of commerce and traffic, but remain deaf to the music of higher spheres.

If we would only know
How you call upon us in the outcry of a fellow man,
The piercing wail of a bereft human being,
The whimpering of a little child.
If we would only know
That each appeal is a gift to us,
A golden opportunity
To console pained members of your body.
If we would only know
How our soul is paralyzed by our plodding life
Full of chatter, idle dreams and warped desires
That drive us from your lovely sight.
If we would only know
How close you are to us,
It would thaw the chill that kills our joy,
The stubborn will that drives us
Like an angry ticking clock
Standing watch against an empty wall.
No longer would our hearts be shallow, small
Logged with sentiments of an angry past
Like a silted harbor cut off from the clear sea
Of your rushing love.

STAYING WITH GRACE

"You have no bucket, sir," she answered, "and the well is deep: how could you get this living water?" (Jn. 4:11-12).

Jesus tried gently to lift his talk with the Samaritan woman to a higher plane. He told her about living waters from which he would let her drink if only she would ask for them. He tried to show her that she was in touch with the saving Lord, the Living Water, the One who refreshes and makes new.

In the Gospel of St. John, we find the beautiful images of bread, water, light, life, of a vine upon which we are grafted like a branch. In each of them, the Evangelist speaks to our heart in search of Jesus. He wants to tell us in striking figures about the gift of Jesus' own life to us. Jesus is the miraculous bread that nurses us back to health. He is the water that refreshes our dried up spirit, our bored mind, our distant heart. He is light in our darkness, life of our life, the precious vine in which we are implanted tenderly by his Father.

St. John knows how overwhelmed we are by daily cares, how fascinated by futile things, how immersed in a make believe world of ambition and self im-

portance that veils for us the true meaning of Jesus'
words. St. John consoles us by showing that even those
who met him in the flesh, who heard his voice, who
looked into his eyes did not understand at once what
he was trying to say. He records faithfully the failure
of people to apprehend the words of Jesus. For
example, the misunderstanding of Nicodemus and
some of the apostles at the last supper. In the woman
at the well, we witness the same lack of comprehension. *"You have no bucket, sir,"* she answered,
*"and the well is deep: how could you get this living
water?"*

The woman is as blindly immersed in everyday
knowledge as we are. Her practical mind knows about
buckets, the depth of a well, and how much cord one
needs to get the bucket down to the water line. Her
practical insight is well developed. What is un-
derdeveloped is her spirit. She seems blind to symbolic
meanings, to the language of the spirit. Like her we
may have a fine sense for the useful. That is a
blessing. Without it our day becomes chaotic. What
would restrict our life dangerously, however, would be
only practical apprehension of reality. We have to
balance this view with a deeper symbolic or mystical
one—a vision that inserts our practical deeds in a
wider context, that gives a deeper motivation to what
we are doing or suffering. It is spirituality that can
keep alive in us the deeper significance of things and
events, of symbolic meanings that go beyond their
immediate usefulness.

It is difficult for the woman at the well to shift from

concrete everyday meanings to the symbolic ones Jesus is pointing to. Hers is our problem too. Seeing his kindness for her, we feel like saying to him:

"It consoles us, Lord, that you do not give up. You keep speaking kindly to the woman in spite of her density; you keep touching her inwardly until the light of insight dawns. Your patience consoles us; it deepens our trust that you will not give up on us in spite of our thick-headedness. Please, Lord Jesus, don't let us down. Stay with us patiently as you did with the woman at the well. Give us the grace to stay with you even if we don't immediately grasp what you are telling us in the depths of our heart.

Your patience, Lord, teaches us something else. There have been moments in our life when you asked us to bring your good tidings to others. How often have we met Samaritans among them, people so occupied with daily cares, with success and possession, that they were not able to understand in the least what we were talking about. We met the Samaritan woman, but we did not have your patience toward her. How tempted we were to give up, to throw in the towel. When such moments come again, grace us with your own patience, your fidelity to the will of the Father, who sent you to this woman as he sends us to others with your message of love and redemption."

The woman goes on: *"Are you a greater man than our father Jacob who gave us this well and drank from it himself with his sons and his cattle?"* (Jn. 4:12).

Jacob, the patriarch of Israel, was highly revered by the simple Samaritans living around the well. In her question the woman raises the possibility that this unusual man talking to her with such dignity might be greater than Jacob—if he is able to give living water without using a bucket or any other instrument. That she can even utter such an unheard of possibility seems to indicate a first touch of grace. There seems to be a slight awakening to the fact that this man Jesus may be someone special, comparable to the patriarch, perhaps surpassing him. Interior grace has begun its transforming action. All depends now on her staying with Jesus. If she leaves him now, the hesitant flicker of light may be extinguished before it could become a flame. She will have missed the best chance of her life.

"How often, Lord, did you light a spark of insight in my distracted mind? It may have been during spiritual reading, a sermon, Holy Mass. Or perhaps it happened at a moving moment of my life: the loss of a beloved one, the birth of a child, falling in love, marriage. Or it might have been during a beautiful concert, a striking movie, a meaningful lecture, during the solitude of sickness and suffering. Your grace affected me, but I did not stay with you as the woman did. I did not allow the little light to grow in me. I did not dwell on the word that touched me, on the inner voice that seemed to speak to me almost inaudibly. I did not treasure every word of yours in my heart as Mary did. I went away from you mindlessly. I threw myself back in countless petty occupations. I did not cherish the small moment of truth in my life. I lost you before I really knew what you had to say to me. Let this not happen again. Let me be tuned in to the tender beginnings of your divine inspiration. Make me still at such moments, recollected inwardly to give your grace a full chance to expand itself in my interiority."

The woman not only stays with Jesus; she begins to pay attention to his words. Her irritation has melted away; she shows respect by now calling him, sir. One thing seems to strike her especially. She begins to realize that this stranger does not care for himself any longer; he seems only concerned about her. To her astonishment he has reversed the situation. He began by asking for a drink casually. He ends up by offering her to drink from miraculous waters without speaking any longer about drinking himself in spite of his thirst. Grace begins to make her inwardly ready for the experience of Jesus' infinite selfless care for any person in need of his love.

> *Jesus replied:*
> *"Whoever drinks this water*
> *will get thirsty again;*
> *but anyone who drinks the water that I shall give*
> *will never be thirsty again:"* (Jn. 4:13-14).

In the beginning of his talk Jesus had done for this woman what he lovingly does for every beginner on the spiritual path. He had mellowed her mood by his grace; he had softened her mind; he had made her more docile, still and attentive to his word. Docility is the great gift of Jesus to beginners.

Now he can reveal to her more about the mysterious water he already is giving her inwardly. He tells her that this water will satisfy her deepest thirst. She begins to experience a silent yearning for the Divine. Like us, she has refused to know that inner thirst, that restless desire. We repress the awareness of it because we are unable to bear with the terrible craving for God that eats away at our hearts. We can only admit it to ourselves when we see a possibility of its relief, an oasis on the horizon of the desert of our life. We live desperately dispersed lives in order to escape the inner yearning. We do everything possible to fill the void inside yet we pass blindly by the only possibility for fulfillment: our Lord Jesus.

Jesus deals gently with every human being. He does not overwhelm anyone with his light and his love. He gently disposes and readies man for that brightness of the light of grace each one is able to bear in his life. He gradually transforms the person he loves. There are many steps along the way. Each step is marked by an infinite respect for our freedom. Each transformation begins not as an imposition but as an invitation. Each grace falls softly from the Divine Tree onto my heart. like a hesistant little seed. If the ground is frozen, if my heart is harsh and closed, the little seed will die under the icy crust of selfishness.

Every grace is an invitation to open my heart, to welcome him graciously. If I am faithful to the first small grace Jesus tries to give me, he will enrich me further. His first grace was necessary to transform me sufficiently for the next one to come. In this way he wants me to grow from grace to grace, from transformation to transformation.

In the measure I respond to these graces, I will be changed inwardly until he has divinized me enough to let me dwell in the fullness of his presence in so far as that is possible here on earth for the limited person I am. In the end he may no longer measure his gifts. He may give himself with an abundance and profusion which surpasses understanding.

This is his way with the woman. He transforms her inwardly in the measure of her inner mellowing under the warmth of his love and his light. He disposes her more and more docilely that he might give her greater lights. That is why he tried to make her see—*"You and others drink from the waters of the earth at this well. You may drink as much as you want; it cannot quench the craving of your inner self. But the living water I bring is of another kind. You who drink of the water I give will no longer be pained by the thirst for a glimpse of the Eternal in your life. You will see; you will hope; you will love in a whole new way. Eternal meaning will have been restored to your daily endeavors."*

Staying with grace is staying with you, my Lord,
The One who refreshes and makes new my day,
Who lessens my fascination with futile things
And awakens me to what only counts.
Keep touching me inwardly until the light of insight dawns.
Do not allow the flicker of light to die
Before it becomes a living flame consuming me.
Make me treasure the dawn that grows in me,
Make me dwell on the voice that speaks inaudibly,
Make me cherish the moment of illumination,
Attune me to the tender beginnings of your inspiration.
Oasis in the wasteland of my life,
Still the noise of daily chatter
That I may hear anew the murmur of the living waters
Running through the universe.
Mellow me, refine my receptivity
That I may surrender graciously
To the blessings you bestow on me.
Let me hear your invitation whispered gently like the rains
of spring.
Give me an angel's wing to rise with you, Eternal Lord,
To light the shadows of this dying earth
With candles of compassion.

GRACE AND SELF TRANSFORMATION

Whoever drinks this water
will get thirsty again;
but anyone who drinks the water that I shall give
will never be thirsty again: [Jn. 4:14].

Jesus often calls his presence food and drink. He wants to impress on us that without him we cannot survive in the life of grace. No sparkle of divine life can be kindled by our own attempts. We are empty vessels to be filled by the Lord. To be filled with the life of Jesus in accordance with who we deeply are is the Christian definition of self fulfillment. This fulfillment will find completion in the Eschaton. As St. John tells us: "We will be like Him." (1 Jn. 3:2). Already here, however, through faith we can delight in a beginning of the splendor which will be ours in the life to come. Our faith inspires us to participate in the unfolding of a redeemed humanity. The living water that Jesus gives strengthens us to build communities of justice and love as radiant pointers to the eternal fulfillment to which humanity is called.

To grow in that life of faith we must tend toward God's presence with our whole heart and will, with all our desires and forces. We must hunger and thirst for his kingdom on earth to be as it is in heaven. Each human being has been created with this hunger for God. In the situation of human innocence before the fall, man tended ceaselessly toward God, gently centering his daily life in him, celebrating and perfecting the earth as a temple of his glory. The fall of man marked the loss of this centeredness. Man attempted to be like God by his own power. Life was no longer a spontaneous celebration of the Presence that fills the universe. Fallen man began to celebrate his own presence. Anxious about his own importance, he wanted to play the role of god or hero in his own right. Life became an idolatry of the ego, a competitive struggle between tense individuals grasping for possessions, status, fame and power.

No matter what man did to fulfill himself, the void that the Eternal created in his heart did not disappear. This void keeps crying out. The cry can be silenced. Yet at times the void makes itself felt again. It rekindles our thirst for the Divine; we suffer again the mystery of our endless restlessness.

The lie of self reliance never covers up totally the hollowness that gnaws at the core of our existence. This void in the center of human life is symbolized in the Gospel of St. John by hunger and thirst. These words express in vital terms how our spirit craves to fill the inner emptiness.

As fallen people we are unable, without grace, to fully realize what we hunger after. Since the fall we live in forgetfulness of how the hunger of the spirit can be stilled or how its mysterious thirst can be quenched. We rightly seek for fulfillment, but we seek it in the wrong places. We fracture our hunger and thirst in countless desires that tear us apart. Before the fall, man tended naturally in all his desires toward God. This healing tendency has been interrupted by sinfulness.

To focus our dispersed desires, to help us see what we are ultimately hungry and thirsty for, our Lord comes to live among us. He himself becomes the fulfillment of man, the consolation of our wounded soul, the living water for our burning thirst.

When we seek fulfillment anywhere else, we meet with disappointment; soon we are thirsty again. That is why Jesus said in so many words to the woman: *"You speak about the water that wells up from the bowels of the earth. You may drink from it as much as you like; soon you will be thirsty again. But he who drinks the water I give will not thirst any more. I am the living water. The person who allows me to enter into his interiority and to permeate his sterile life, as living water revitalizes the desert, will feel revived; he will bloom and bear precious fruit. He will be less misled by small desires. His thirst will be quenched partly in this life, fully in the life to come."*

We should see the difference between a life of dispersed desire and a life of longing for the Eternal. The more we are graced by him, the more we long for him. The measure of our longing is the measure of our love. The graced life of divine longing is different from the life of fragmented desires pulling us in opposite directions.

Graced longing arises from a gift already received, from inner abundance, not from emptiness, as do our frantic desires for countless things. The longing self is graced already with God's loving presence; it is tasting his entrancing Truth and Beauty. The self is enflamed with longing, with graced desires.

In this sense desire is not diminished but deepened in the self that drinks the living water. Different human desires are not drowned by the living water. They become less dispersed, less unruly. The Christian who drinks the water of the Lord begins to experience the eternal horizon beyond all limited views of his particular desires. In and through these limited horizons, he begins to orient himself toward the radiant horizon of Everlasting Love.

The life of dispersed desires is disturbing. Not so the new life of graced longing for the living water. This longing is filled with spiritual delights unknown to the senses. For the deepest self, thus graced, possesses already what it is tending after; it tends joyfully after more of the same. This spiritual tending harmonizes and unifies all vital and personal desires. It offers a passionate and beautiful mindfulness of one thing only: the God of love. This oneness of ultimate desire gives peace and unity to the human self on its mysterious journey to the Source from which it emerged.

Sometimes the inner presence hides itself. Then the

longing is pierced with pain. But the pains of divine love and longing carry a mystical delight that the self would not exchange for anything in the world of the senses. This delight of the mystic self in darkness wells up from the naked awareness in faith that a graced Presence engulfs one's life with limitless love.

The mystic life of longing for the Eternal, with its pains and delights, does not diminish the Christian commitment to humanity and its liberation. The inner light purifies and intensifies this engagement. For the Presence of the most High is experienced not only as an abyss of entrancing beauty and love to lose oneself in; it is also experienced as a call, as a divine invitation to stand up, to be counted as Moses, the prophets and Jesus were, as an invitation to cope with daily life situations and to discover in that coping the unique contribution the self is meant from eternity to make to the unfolding of a redeemed humanity.

> . . . *the water that I shall give*
> *will turn into a spring inside him, welling up*
> *to eternal life.*

The living water that Jesus gives is like a spring inside us. We carry it with us; it is always ready to well up. It refreshes and strengthens us in our daily endeavors with humanity to build the earth and the kingdom of God. The more we allow this living water to quench our thirst for worship and human service, the more it wells up inwardly. When we are called to leave the earth we helped to perfect in our own little way, the spring inside us does not leave us. Now it will well up in us to eternal life. The thirst of our spirit will be quenched throughout eternity. The inner well becomes the source of our participation in God's glory.

The graces of our Lord are not mere adornments of our deepest self or spirit. They transform that self, render it new and radiant, set it on the road toward divine fulfillment. The holiness of our Lord permeates our spirit self as a fine perfume permeates the stale air of a dusty room. The Lord endows this poor self with his own attitudes and dispositions. They become really ours. We change substantially in the melting fire of grace without knowing it. We are not the same as we were before. The spring of living water inside us has truly changed us into Jesus; such is the mystery of transforming participation. Yet this gradual metamorphosis of the self is done with infinite respect for what we already are in God's plan by birth and background.

The mighty water of a river bends and twists itself in adaptation to the fundamental form of the canyon it streams through. Yet it polishes and streamlines the walls of the canyon it touches daily. Similarly the living water of grace welling up inside us adapts itself to the fundamental form God gave to our deepest self. Yet it gently washes away the dirty spots, the rough edges, the dark shadows that mar the original beauty God intended from eternity for this unique self. He makes us more and more like he intended us to be in the Eternal Word.

During this life on earth, we cannot see the wonder of our self transformation by the Lord. We can only live and labor in faith and hope. We may realize that we are dying to the dominance of our ego self. But the resurrection of the new graced form of our deepest self is hidden, as it were, under the veil of faith. At our death we are liberated from the vitalistic and personalistic dimensions of our selfhood. During our life on earth they supported and linked our deepest self with daily reality. At the same time they veiled and obscured this self. Death takes them away. So too the veil of faith falls away the moment we enter into the life of glory. At that instant the whole splendor of the Lord in our transformed self will reveal itself. We will see in eternal gratefulness how the inner spring of grace made our deepest self similar to Jesus. We will see how the spring inside us leaps up with dazzling splendor for all eternity. It makes us other Christs sharing the splendor of the Father's glory.

"The just will shine like the sun in the reign of their Father" (Mt. 13:43), for their deepest lasting self has been transformed by participation in the Sun that Jesus is.

A void, a hollowness,
A child in agony
Cries out in me.
The wonder of your living water
May resurrect this hollow life,
Make it bloom again,
Make it bear fruit.
Fill my emptiness with longing
To lose myself in your abyss.
Longing may be pierced with pain,
But pain of love is sweet to bear
As long as there is faith and trust
That Brother Sun went into hiding
To reappear more radiantly
When night is gone.
Let your river streamline
My resistant life, dull the edges
Of this canyon, worn and ragged,
Mellow bitterness that mars the beauty
Meant for me from all eternity.
Let your river be a spring in me
Leaping up in dazzling splendor
The moment I awake in Everlasting Life.

THE BEGINNING OF NEW LIFE

"Sir, said the woman, "give me some of that water, so that I may never get thirsty and never have to come here again to draw water" (Jn. 4:15).

Jesus had spoken softly about the mystery of the living water, its potency to rejuvenate a human life withering away in trivia. He had touched her mind, her heart, her whole being. He had disclosed the truth compassionately in a simple way—the way of everyday image and metaphor so that his message might tie in with things and work familiar to her, things such as drawing water from the well, water to wash with, to drink from, sparkling water to keep alive man, animal and plant.

She was strangely moved by the mysterious dignity and peace of this weary traveller. She was thrilled by something invisible, something infinitely worthwhile and deep behind his simple and melodious words. Yet she was unable to grasp what he was saying. Like any human self immersed in petty concerns, she could not open up all at once to the fullness of divine truth, to the blinding radiance of the horizon of the Infinite.

Grace must slowly drive its golden wedge into the shut up human self, barricaded by countless defenses.

If the self is faithful to the shaft of light piercing through from grace, new graces will pour in, provided the self does not resist them. The living waters will then hasten the moment when the fully opened self dwells radiantly in the unapproachable light. Ultimate fullness will come only in the hereafter. Yet we are called to ready ourselves for this fullness by approaching it increasingly in the daily here and now.

For the woman, the words of the Lord accompanied by interior graces have illumined a little the dimness of her closed off self. Slowly grace begins to convert her dispersed being to its hidden depth in the Eternal Word.

Necessary for fuller conversion is the growth of an inner yearning for what Jesus offers, a growth so lustrous that it fills the whole self with longing love. To plant the tiny seed of that longing, Jesus had begun to give her a foretaste of the power and beauty of the living water that he would like to well up in her as his personal gift. His words and inward graces had not been in vain. She feels surging up in her desolate self a longing filled with love for the living water. She cannot withhold her desire. In an effusion of love for the Lord, she begs him: *"Sir, give me some of that water . . . "*

Her further words show that her affection for him is strangely mixed with self love, as it is in all beginners in the life of the spirit. The first spiritual lights are full of shadows. Her words, *"so that I may never . . . have to come here again to draw water",* show self interest, subtly blended with genuine longing for the gift of

God. Her qualified request betrays her eagerness to get rid of the burdensome toil of getting water from the well. The newly lit spark of heavenly wisdom is hemmed in by the shadows of a worldly cleverness she had been at home with for so long. She can only conceive of living water in some mundane way.

We feel moved by her predicament. It sounds familiar to us. It strikes home. We are even more moved by the patience and kindness of our Lord. We need his patience so badly ourselves. This need makes us pray:

"Lord, we too are like the woman at the well. Often we are moved by your grace. We long then to live for you alone, yet countless thin threads keep us fastened to a web of petty concerns and selfish designs. We want to give ourselves to you, to withhold nothing, yet we are too attached to small satisfactions to really let go. Like the Samaritan woman, we are secretly figuring out: 'What may be in it for us? Is it not costing too much?' Small-minded, are we, like keepers of a religious grocery store."

"Lord, Jesus, pour into us more and more of the living water of grace so that we may be satisfied enough to let go of our hold on fleeting praises and pleasures. We cling to them so desperately, as if our life depends on them. We run around nervously seeking to quench our secret thirst. In our agitation we miss out on your water of grace. More thirsty than ever, we begin to gulp avidly from the deadly polluted streams of power, status, possession. Lord, give us your clean living water that the thirst of our deepest self may be quenched, that we may be weaned away from our addiction to the murky waters of worldliness."

Like most people at the beginning of the spiritual life, the woman has little insight into her inner feelings and motives. She needs the direction of Jesus to clarify her inner confusion. Ignorant in the way of the spirit, she is not yet able to appraise rightly human and graced sentiments. It is true she senses a graced longing deep down in herself. But in her confused interiority—still filled with an array of worldly concerns—the graced longing becomes blended with selfish desires. She is still too much anchored in childish fantasies, in the idle hope of finding paradise on earth. She ends up proclaiming mainly the selfish side of her mixed, confused longing. She was unable to put into words the hesitant beginning of a whole new kind of graced longing of which she could have only a vague and shadowy awareness.

Again how very much like us she is. We too are ignorant regarding what we want. We imagine so often that our longing for the Eternal is pure and singleminded. We feel so pleased with our pious self, so righteous about our motives. We fail to recognize that we merely mixed a few golden pellets of graced longing with the old sticky mass of self serving desires and designs. Our graced aspirations are soon polluted; rarely do they remain untainted by our old selves or uncontaminated by this age.

It takes a life long growth in graced awareness to purify them. This awareness, will only be pure in a final sense if Christ himself burns us clean in the dark nights of sense and spirit. But the grace of the dark night, especially the passive nights of sense and spirit, may never be given to us. In the meantime, we might turn our inner pollution into an asset by making it a source of humility. Humility means digging deep holes in our pompous self, calcified by willfulness and pride. Each hole dug by humility leaves room for the Lord and his grace. One means to maintain the power of humility in our soul is the constant awareness that our holiest longings, our best motives, are tainted by selfishness. The golden pellet of holy longing is his gift; its contamination we must claim as our own.

Mystery of Living Water, renew, invigorate
A flimsy mind, a listless heart,
A feeble will, a scattered fantasy
Before this idle life is swept away
Like a useless pebble into a sea
Of trivia.
Let the blinding light of the Infinite
Drive its golden wedge
Into the center of my being.
Let its shaft of love
Pierce my armor until I find
My hidden depth in the Eternal Word.
Fill my self with longing love;
Light a spark of wisdom
Amidst the shadows of my cleverness.
Cut the countless threads
That keep me fastened to a fleeting earth.
Dig holes in my pretentious self
Calcified by willfulness and pride.
Make me aware
That the golden pellet of holy longing,
Though mixed with selfish sentiment,
Is a most precious and undeserved gift.
Mine only is its contamination.

GRACE AND DETACHMENT

The woman asked Jesus for living water with longing love. He was willing to give it to her, as he is ready to grant us the graces we need. We may not be ready to receive his gifts. Graces we are not ready to receive are like lost seeds falling among weeds that smother their life giving power, that stunt their unfolding. How, then, does the self become a receptive ground for grace?

To become ready for grace, we need a growing awareness that our search for fulfillment outside of God has been in vain, that it has wounded us. We need the insight that idle pursuits have led us to idolize people and things. We substituted them for God, displacing him as the ultimate source of joy and meaning. This awareness may give rise to humility and repentance, two sure means to clean up our inner garden, to ready it for the seeds of grace and for their fruitful sprouting in our lives.

Humbleness must pervade our wounded self as a fine fragrance, making us as attractive to God as a demure bride is for her groom. An atmosphere of repentance must create and gently maintain a movement of inner distancing from self-created idols and the frenzied agitation they evoke. These "little beyonds" we create as substitutes for the Eternal are weeds that suffocate the tender shoots of grace in our garden. No matter what we do to get rid of them, such weeds seem to show up persistently. That is why we need to tear them out over and over again in patient love. Then the weeds may diminish enough to allow the seeds of grace to sprout forth freely and flourish.

The gardeners of our spiritual life—awareness of idle pursuits, unmasking of idols, humbleness, and repentance—are needed by the Samaritan woman also. Jesus wants to give her the living water she is asking for, but he knows his grace will be a lost treasure, a gift in vain, as long as the weeds are not cut in the unkempt garden of her life. Gently he begins to awaken the sleepy gardeners in her soul. Jesus is always ready to awaken us; we are seldom ready for him. Our small minds are immersed in petty concerns; we are too earth bound to sense what Jesus is talking about. We are hunting for fulfillment in the wrong places, running eagerly after the wrong pipers. Our hearts and minds must be shaken loose from their rusty moorings in worldly routines. We must be shamed by the shallowness of our sinful lives. Perhaps the Lord may bless us with an event that shakes us out of the narrow niches we have dug so laboriously for ourselves. The blessing of inner upheaval often brings the grace of sudden self-awareness. We are brought face to face with the forlornness of a life without the Lord. Jesus graces the woman at the well with this gift of self recognition.

"Go and call your husband" said Jesus to her "and come back here." The woman answered, "I have no husband." He said to her: "You are right to say, 'I have no husband'; for although you have had five, the one you have now is not your husband. You spoke the truth there" (Jn. 4:17-18).

She had been hunting for human happiness outside the mystery of the Divine. She had been sorely disappointed over and over again. Her life was a sad succession of vain pursuits of human fulfillment. How often she must have said to her tired and empty self with a final sigh of relief: "This is really it. At last I have captured the flighty bird of happiness, never to let it go." Her hand closed anxiously around this small creature, but, alas, the song had already died in the little bird. Soon enough she found that he too had perished in her gripping fingers like all the others before him. Joy cannot be caught. It is a gift that comes and goes in its own time.

How impossible it seems to be to admit that one's life has been in vain—impossible when there is no alternative on the horizon. But Jesus is this alternative. Once we meet him as our savior, we gladly admit that life without him was a sordid mistake, a dreary affair. It works also the other way around. The recognition of the lostness of a life outside the Divine readies us for an intimate meeting with Jesus. Usually the two graces work together: the grace of recognition of human emptiness and the grace of recognition of Jesus' fullness and forgiveness.

St. John, a master of the life of divine grace, shows

these two divine operations at work in the Samaritan woman. Jesus had made himself already known to her by his words and by graces that moved her inwardly. Her interiority was not yet ready for a fuller revelation. She understands very little of who he is, of what he is offering to her. She is still too immersed in the things of this world. Jesus grants her the grace of recognizing the emptiness of a mere human search for happiness. While illuminating her mind with his words, he also keeps giving himself to her inner life. He gives her inwardly the grace of recognizing him as the full and forgiving presence of the Father. Soon after giving her the grace of a sweet upheaval of her worldly mind, he will reveal even more about who he is. He will in fact make her his first missionary among the Samaritan people.

Jesus wants the woman to realize how useless her pursuit of happiness has been. He hopes that the grace of this insight will make her more ready for the living water he desires to give. At the same time he wants her to grow to a deeper awareness of who he is by showing what miraculous knowledge he has of her life. By his words, and the inner graces that go with them, he has already disposed her for the revelation that her life failed to find a lasting meaning.

The Divine Love manifests an incomparable gentleness even when we are carried away by our attachments to the things of this world. How tactfully he readies this simple woman for full encounter with his love. With what mildness does he remind her of the painful past so that she might see how futile her life has been so far. There is no reproach, no threat, no sign of repulsion or rejection, only a quiet remembrance of the facts of her life, leaving it up to her to come to a final conclusion. How respectful of her freedom Jesus is. He does not coerce her by playing on her anxieties or by showing a heavy hand. He leaves it all up to her. "These are the facts of your life," he seems to say. "This is the offer of my love. Here is my grace of enlightenment. It is up to you to decide freely which way to go."

In a mild way, he reminds her of her idle pursuit of happiness in five marriages, of the men who were her past and present idols. In the wake of this new awareness, he begins to instill in her the softening attitudes of repentance and humility. They will plough the frozen ground of her hidden self and help dig the open furrows in which the seeds of grace may fall. Soon she will taste the sweetness of repentance.

How can repentance be sweet? Repentance is the awareness of forgiveness in the midst of sorrow. It occasions relief from pretentions that cramp our life style, that make us think we can stand tall by the power of our imagined excellence. Repentance relieves us from the constant strain to make ourselves and others believe in our innocence. No longer do we have to convince ourselves that we are not sinners like the rest of men. We admit who we are and repent, resting our restless hearts in the goodness and forgiveness of Jesus.

Our Lord makes the woman see that each of her former husbands had become an idol in her life—all fallen—and that the same may happen to the man she lives with now. He shows her the vain dream of expecting from these lovers the fulfillment that only God can give. This idle expectation had driven her from liaison to liaison. Jesus tells her these things to strengthen her wavering faith by showing what miraculous knowledge he has of her life.

What a risk it was for him as a stranger to enter uninvited into the delicate secrets of the life of this woman. She could have felt insulted. After all she did not know who he was. She could have taken his questions and remarks as crude prying, uncalled for in a passing traveller. She could have withdrawn from him in indignation, curtly closing off further conversation.

But the adorable presence of our Lord, his words full of grace and light, his ineffable goodness, the inner graces inviting her softly to faith, hope and love draw her to him in such a way that she is able to bear this painful confrontation with the past he is exposing to her. His way of attaching someone to himself worked in her without her being aware of it. She did not know who he was, nor did she understand well his divine communications. Mellowed by the inner and outer graceful presence of Jesus, however, the woman takes no offense when he reveals to her that he knows about the five husbands that were hers and about the man she is living with presently.

This incident might tell us about our own search for satisfaction. Each lost human self may have its own story of five or more husbands. We may have been wedded to fame and glory, to the gang, the in-group, the community, to money and success, to popularity, pleasure and power, to some social cause. We may have tried out some or all of them to find ultimate happiness and meaning in life. We may not have realized what we were doing. But the Lord knows, for he knows the innermost recesses of the human heart. Suddenly his grace may touch us, incite us to confront ourselves and our unholy liaisons. At the same time he deepens in us the faith, hope and love that may carry us through such a crisis of self discovery. When aware of sin and failure we must ask him to deepen our faith, hope and love. Without this deepening we may no longer feel able to respond to the painful grace of awareness. It may be a consolation to know that the grace of crisis and the humility and repentance it gives rise to is usually granted at the beginning of a period of deepening in the spiritual life.

"Go and call your husband," said Jesus to her, *"and come back here."* Jesus is the exquisite master of encounter. He begins with an innocent invitation that would not threaten or compel her. His invitation is so worded that it gives her a chance to hide from him or to show her growing faith by not concealing the truth. She has been touched enough by grace to open up to him. She tells him that she has no husband. She did not yet know that our Lord knew the secrets of the heart; still something in her inclined her to be honest with him. While inviting her to go and call her husband, the Lord inspired her with good sentiments. He prompted her inwardly to be at ease with him

about her life. The adorable presence of our Lord, his words full of grace, his ineffable gentleness and the interior inspirations of love he gave her to draw her to himself did indeed attract her in a holy manner. His way of attracting someone to himself worked in her without her being aware of it and she did not know who he was nor did she understand well what he was leading up to.

He said to her, "You are right to say, 'I have no husband'; for although you have had five, the one you have now is not your husband. You spoke the truth here."

If we open up to Jesus, he opens up even more to us. Nobody can outdo him in generosity. She had been forthright with him and he told her kindly that she had spoken the truth. He rewards her with a revelation of his divine knowledge of her life. Not hearing personally his words, we do not know what they sounded like. From the rest of the story, however, from her pleased and relaxed response, we gather that his tone must have been one of utmost compassion. She must have felt deeply his understanding, his forgiveness, his tender comprehension of her painful predicament. She needed so much to believe in him. To strengthen her hesitant faith, he showed her his miraculous knowledge of her life.

The Lord speaks to us in our life situation; this is the well where we meet him daily. In and through the situation he may invite us to give something up that is dear to us. He offers a challenge to unfold our graced Christian life. If, with the Samaritan woman, we say yes to this call, we emerge as a new self in Christ. As Christians on the way, we choose a new self that approaches a little more the divine direction meant for us from eternity. We bury the old self fixated on one "husband" after another but we rise anew in Christ. Jesus tries to convince us, as he convinced the woman at the well that he has our best interests at heart. If we trust in the Lord as she finally did, he will reveal to us our graced possibilities for growth in him. He may use any inner or outer means to shake us loose from our routines and attachments. Awakening may happen at such unusual moments of experience as the loss of dear ones, illness, unexpected changes in church and society, unemployment, the challenge of a new career, marital crises, awareness of new talents, needs, ideals, falling in love, social failure and success. Such changes may cause us to question our current self. Our current self comprises the usual ways in which we perceive and approach God and people and ourselves in relation to them. Like the woman at the well we too may be shaken loose from everything we believed we could humanly count on.

At such times our life may seem almost catastrophic. We may not know where to turn. We may believe that its foundation is shattered. The shake up may be so strong that it becomes impossible for us to retreat comfortably to what used to be. The woman meeting Jesus had reached a point of no return. She could no longer experience the joy of going back in a relaxed and unperturbed way to her past life. Her self image is changed irrevocably under the impact of the perception evoked by Jesus.

The same may happen to us when we meet Jesus at our well. The change in our self image granted by his grace can be denied or repressed but not obliterated. To deny the new image he gives us, we have to harden our hearts. In that case our state after we meet Jesus is worse than it was before we were graced with this encounter. It is the greatness of the Samaritan woman that she can say yes to the self perception Jesus gives her. This awareness becomes for her a source of new life.

Make my heart less earthbound, Lord,
My mind less drowned in small designs.
Let me run no longer after the seductive pipers
Of this small and narrow land
Of lust and arrogance.
Shake me loose from my rusty moorings
In worldly routines.
Shame me by the shallowness
Of a lost and empty life,
A sad succession of pursuits
Of earthly happiness.

Anxiously I hunted for fulfillment,
Evading me like a lark in flight.
When I thought I captured it,
The song had choked already
In its little throat.
Soon the graceful singer died.
I clutched only a bunch of feathers
In my grasping hand.

Grant the grace of sweet upheaval
To this dense and dreary life.
Let me meet you at the well of daily happenings
As once the woman did.
Create a new heart in me
That I may not return blindly
To all that used to be.

JESUS, THE PROPHET

"I see you are a prophet, sir" said the woman (Jn. 4:19).

Grace begins to penetrate the woman's spirit. She receives a first illumination about Jesus. He is not yet for her the Messiah, surely not the Son and Image of the Father. But neither is he any longer a mere traveller, a passing Jew from Galilee, a remarkable stranger. Grace makes her "see" that he is a prophet. This seeing is not due simply to the fact that he has shown her a miraculous knowledge of the secrets of her life. This feat corroborates her first enlightenment about Jesus. The loving intuition itself has a deeper ground, that of grace. It is neither the result of reasoning nor of human sentiment. Any "seeing" of Jesus, with the inner eye of the spirit, is a gift we cannot force, deserve or reason to. It is a graced intuition, at once there at the heart of the searching self.

"I see you are a prophet." A prophet is not merely a person who may tell the future or manifest knowledge of one's hidden past or present. Such signs may authenticate the prophet's mission, but they do not constitute the mission itself. Predictions of the future, striking insights into the secrets of one's life, are

startling. We think immediately of such "spectaculars" when we hear the word prophet. But to see with the inner eye that a person is a prophet is to be aware that he truly stands and speaks for God, that he is a unique mediator, that he dwells in the twilight between humanity and divinity. Out of this twilight, he speaks the message of God to mankind.

Prophets were the highest manifestation of the Divine known to this woman. She knew about their existence long ago from the history of the chosen people. She would never have dared to dream the impossible: that she, a simple and sinful woman of Sychar, a poor Samaritan despised by Israel, would personally meet with a new prophet of the living God. She could not have imagined this event would happen to her; even now she doubts it. But at once the light is there, overflowing her spirit. She "sees" he is a prophet.

Jesus is *the* prophet, *the* mediator without peer. As prophet he is called to speak to the community of believers of all times. He speaks in the name of God also to each of the faithful, to each of us, as he does to the Samaritan woman. The prophet Jesus, as the Eternal Word, reveals what the Father has willed for us from eternity as our unique life direction. He communicates to our deepest self how to follow him in our own way. The prophet, Jesus, mediates between God's eternal plan over our lives and our living out of this plan in time and space.

I may meet Jesus, the prophet, in my own experience and in the proclamation of the Church, in scripture, sacraments, liturgy and spiritual masters. Enlightening me as prophet, he enables me to approximate my unique life direction. Our destiny is contained in Christ, for we are contained in him as little words in the Eternal Word. Our deepest self is hidden in Christ and Christ is hidden in God. The prophetic speaking of Christ in us is the gradual revelation of our life direction hidden in him.

Christ is *the* prophet, *the* mediator, because he is the eternal expression of God's unique plan as well as the human model and example of how we should live and incarnate this divine project in daily life. Listening to the prophet, Jesus, leads to transformation: a change of the person in his inmost being, a transfiguration that will find its perfection in the eschaton when each faithful Christian will share in the glorification of his Lord.

When I grow to the fullness of spiritual life, Christ will no longer be experienced as a prophet separated from me. I will have moments of spontaneous awareness that the prophet is in me, that I am in him. Deep in me the divine prophet begins to speak in the welling up of attitudes that are consonant with my eternal self. The prophet Jesus communicates to my whole life and being what the unique direction of my life should be. This is the deepest form of prophesy. My whole life direction, all my deeds, feelings, willing and planning, begin to flow from Jesus' silent prophesying in the center of my self. The prophet Jesus wants to reveal to me my eternal selfhood as he tries with great love and patience to reveal it to the simple, sinful woman at Jacob's well.

Thaw the tundra of my soul,
Uproot the weeds that choke your gift.
Till the soil, dig the furrows
In which your grace may softly sink
To weather the winter of my heart.
Do not allow your grace in me
To dwindle like seed
Choked off by weeds
That suffocate and drain its power.
Let me gather sweetness from your flowers
In the garden of my soul.
Let my ear remain attuned
To your silent voice of Love
O prophet of my destiny,
O infinite sea that carries me.
Let my life flow forth
From your prophetic call
In the still point of my soul.

THE GRACE OF WORSHIP

The woman is struck by Jesus' power to read her heart, to see into the secrets of her life. She already has called him a prophet. Now she wants him to enlighten her and her people about the most important thing in human life: the worship of the Lord. In the course of this graced conversation, her mind has been elevated from preoccupation with daily chores to that alone which gives meaning and radiance to everything we do: loving worship of him who keeps us and all things in existence.

She wants to find out for sure how God desires to be adored. While the Jewish people had centered their worship in the temple of Jerusalem her own people had built a rival temple on the mountain Gerizim which was destroyed by Hyrcanus. They still centered their worship on this mountain. The woman said to Jesus: *"Our fathers worshiped on this mountain, while you say that Jerusalem is the place where one ought to worship"* (Jn. 4:20).

The way in which she asked him seems to indicate receptivity and docility for anything Jesus will teach her, that inner readiness of a graced soul who finally surrenders to her Master. Jesus rewards such docility with great gifts of insight. He will not restrict himself to an immediate answer to her question; he will go far beyond it, announcing to her the new and unexpected kind of worship he as the high priest of mankind will enkindle in those who will participate in his own life of worship of the Father.

Jesus said: *"Believe me, woman, the hour is coming when you will worship the Father neither on this mountain nor in Jerusalem"* (Jn. 4:21).

The Lord is going to manifest himself and his mission to her and to us—a world wide mission of worship so at odds with the confined religious thought of both Samaritans and Jews that it would seem unbelievable to this simple woman. Indeed it would be impossible for any person in Israel to comprehend the depth and the universality of the new worship of the Father in Christ all mankind would be called to in this gentle stranger now speaking to her. He can only hope that she will wholeheartedly believe even if she cannot understand. Therefore, he begins with the words: *"Believe me, woman,"* and then he announces the future of human worship in him and through him over all the earth. *"The hour is coming when you will worship the Father neither on this mountain nor in Jerusalem."* He hints to her about the miracle of his own worship, living on in his Church, offering God unceasingly himself as a pure and spotless victim.

Jesus is ready to answer directly the woman's question. *"You worship what you do not know; we worship what we do know; for salvation comes from the Jews."* (Jn. 4:22) He does not hide the divine truth, no matter how painful it may sound to this Samaritan woman who loves her own people deeply. He tells her that only the Jewish people have been chosen by God to keep the true faith alive in mankind and to bring forth the one who is the salvation of all peoples. Jesus uses here the word "salvation", a word well known to this woman and to all people in Israel. Yahweh was experienced as salvation, as the one who relieves his people from anxiety, doubt and guilt; he is the rock in which one can trust, who mercifully takes away the sins of the penitent, who returns peace to the downhearted and afflicted.

The Hebrew word for salvation is Yeshu'ah. The word Jesus comes from that. Yeshu'ah has, among other meanings, that of opening up, liberating, making space, setting free, taking away confinement and limitation. Widening the true worship of Israel to all mankind, while deepening it infinitely, is a dimension of salvation, of opening up, of breaking through constrainment.

The Lord is preparing the woman for the revelation that he is the Messiah. Therefore he tells her about a new kind of worship that began already with his coming into the world. *"But the hour will come—in fact it is here already—when true worshipers will worship the Father in spirit and truth; that is the kind of worshiper the Father wants. God is spirit, and those who worship must worship in spirit and truth"* (Jn. 4:23-24).

The coming of our Lord means that a new worship in the spirit of Jesus has become possible for all men, a worship in tune with the revealed truth of God's own inner life. This worship, effected in us by the spirit of Jesus, must be first of all an aspiration of our inmost mind, heart and will. In the core of our being we will be moved by Jesus himself. Only then will the outward expression of our inner adoration be pleasing to God and benefit our spiritual unfolding. Our worship must flow over into our daily life. The life of the true worshiper must be like a candle burning brightly for the Lord. The more we grow in spirit and in truth the more Jesus will take over our worship.

Let us dwell for a while on the spirituality of the true worshiper which Jesus reveals here to the woman. The life of the true worshiper is a joyful celebration of the infinite mystery that no eye has seen and no mind has penetrated. A life of worship means that we submit adoringly all that we are to the originating mystery we call with Jesus "Our Father". The virtue of religion is a virtue of proclaiming, praising, thanking the limitless bounty of God's beauty, truth and goodness. This virtue is at the root of our spiritual life. All we do in daily life should become worship of the Lord. The radiance of our inner worship bestows on all our acts a special orientation; they are more and more directed to praise of the most high.

Because we have received from his bounty all the gifts we enjoy, our worship is not only one of praise but also of gratitude. As true worshipers, we submit to the infinite mystery of love as our beginning and as our destiny. We begin to see the cosmos as created and as steadily unfolding for his glory. We perceive our daily world as a manifestation of his splendor and as a means for our growth into his love and light.

The more humanity grows in a spirituality of worship, the more the Father's loving design in creation is fulfilled. Worship is basically spiritual because only through my spiritual mind and will can I become at one with God, the most pure Spirit. Jesus says, therefore, to the woman at the well: *"God is spirit, and those who worship him must worship in spirit and in truth."* Spiritual worship is the core of any worship acceptable to the Eternal One. As incarnated spiritual persons, we must manifest this depth dimension in exterior acts, for our body must also have its part in the worship that consumes us. Such participation of our vital body in our life of worship is only meaningful because of the spirit it expresses. Our vital life should help us to awaken and foster our spiritual life; it should also enflesh and express the radiance of our interiority which tends to flow over into the lower dimensions of our self. We should thus never be satisfied with a mere external liturgy; it could not please the Lord nor benefit ourselves. Our visible worship should be carried by our invisible presence to the Lord.

Not only should our body participate in our spiritual presence but all the creatures that play a role in our lives. Then we become like priests of the universe. We offer all we touch, see, hear, and sense to the Eternal Mystery that penetrates and surrounds us. We integrate these persons and things in our presence to God. In our worshiping spirit all creatures blend into a unity of adoration, shining forth most brightly the divine destiny of the universe.

Worship is the knowledge and praise of God's glory. This glory God expresses in an Eternal Word, the Divine Word. The splendor of this glory becomes at one with human nature. We all share that nature. It is truly ours and therefore we become the real family of the Eternal Word and, in and through him, the family of the blessed Trinity. We share in divine sonship in him. Made our High Priest, he renders for us perfect praise and glory to God while we are at one with him in his Mystical Body. Our spiritual life is lived in the mystery of his light that, as St. John says, enlightens every one who enters into this world (Jn. 1:29).

God created all things for the adornment of his majesty, that all in unison might give rise to a concert of worship in the Lord Jesus. "Through Him, with Him, in Him in the unity of the Holy Spirit all glory and honor is yours almighty Father for ever and ever." Jesus is the Priest of God's glory at work in all of us. The holy humanity of Jesus is the closest possible tie between the Infinite Mystery and the cosmos that flowed from it, the fullness of the divinity permeates Christ's humanity, consecrating it for a worship infinitely pleasing to the Father. The moment of this incarnation is the moment of his priestly consecration, of sacrifice. Christ had to be the victim of his own sacrifice, a Lamb slain. (Rev. 5:6). The spiritual life of mankind converges on that sacrifice and flows from it. Christian spiritual life is thus a configuration with the priesthood of Jesus, a sharing in his sacrifice, that we may be worshipers of the Father in him in spirit and in truth.

You read my heart, You see the secrets of my life,
My lostness in lust and little things, not harmonized
In loving worship of you alone, my Lord.
O let me be within your loving spotless Son
A worshiper in spirit and in truth.
A candle burning brightly for the Lord.
Turn my days into a joyful celebration
Ot the Mystery that is my origin and end.
Unite me with you, high priest of humanity,
Alpha and Omega, beginning and end,
Firstborn of all creatures.
For you have chosen me
Before the foundation of the world,
You are the vibration of my soul.
Make me a priest of the universe
Blending all creatures inwardly
Into a song of praise and adoration.
Let the radiance of your worship
Shine upon my daily doings.
Change the world before my inner eye
Into a revelation of your splendor,
Shining forth most brightly
The destiny of all that is.

THE SELF REVELATION OF JESUS
TO THE SAMARITAN WOMAN

"The woman said to him, "I know that Messiah—that is, Christ—is coming: and when he comes he will tell us everything" (Jn. 4:25).

The woman could not really fathom all that the Lord was telling her about the new worship in spirit and in truth. Yet she was receiving some deep impression in her soul for her heart had softened during this conversation with Jesus and was already touched by the gift of faith. This gift had made her sufficiently receptive and docile to realize that Jesus was speaking about great and holy things to come. That same faith made her feel serious about his solemn announcement that people would be called to worship in spirit and in truth. She found it easier to understand what was more concrete in his conversation, namely, that people would no longer adore only at Jerusalem or on Mt. Gerizim. But she was not yet purified enough in heart and mind to receive a deeper light of understanding about worship in spirit and truth. Yet what she had heard from him sounded so profound and providential that in her mind she could only connect it with what she knew as most prophetic and exciting for her own future and that of her people. Therefore she said to our Lord in so many words: "You must be speaking about the Messiah who has been promised us; yes, I believe that he will come. And when he has come he will tell us everything we have to do." She seems to imply that she will be ready to do what he asks of her too.

The woman seems not yet aware that Jesus himself is the Messiah so eagerly awaited. Yet his impressive manner and his words, the inner grace that went with them, had already penetrated her soul so deeply that she was ready for his great message. She is an unsophisticated, sinful, socially insignificant woman of the country, very different from the learned and dignified Pharisee Nicodemus, prominent resident of the capital, highly regarded in the leading circles of Judaism. He too had encountered Jesus personally and was touched by him. He was self righteous, a well-known Jew, a member of the chosen people. There was no self righteousness in her and she was not even a Jewess. Yet she gains far more access to Jesus than he did. Self righteousness and pride seem like a screen through which grace cannot easily penetrate. Not that she in any way realized yet that this tired stranger would be the Messiah. Simply, what he had said and the way he had said it brought the Messiah to her mind. Like her people she carried in her weary heart the hope that the Savior would some day come. The hope is vague in regard to the time of his coming. She says, *"When* he comes . . . it may be any time far in the future, who knows?" Crucial, however, for her readiness is that the old hope be rekindled in her heart. The yearning is renewed for the promised One who will tell her what to do to restore peace, joy and meaning to her empty life. He will do even more she says. The Holy One will tell *everything* people would have to know; he will tell it not only to her, but also to all others; indeed he will tell us everything.

St. John adds for his readers in Asia Minor: "Messiah—that is, Christ." This addition of St. John makes us share the feelings of his readers, our brothers and sisters in early Christianity. We feel like participating in their love and adoration when they read the word "Christ." How their deep devotion to his holy humanity must have been aroused while reading the story of his meeting with the woman at the well. How joyfully they carried the name Christians. Christ means the Anointed, which is the original Greek meaning of the word Christos. This name calls up the image of refined aromatic oil penetrating gently what it touches, softening it and filling it with pleasing odor. Was that not what they themselves had experienced in their souls when touched by the Holy Spirit, filling them with profound peace, serenity and abandonment to the Lord? Was Jesus himself not the perfect anointed one, totally filled with the Spirit, the only one who could truly be called the Anointed of God? Was their own experience of anointing by the Spirit, that penetration of their interiority, not a participation in the anointment of Jesus himself, from whom all divine anointment of human souls flows forth? The wonderful story of the gentle divine touch of the soul of this sinful woman must have reminded Christian readers of what happened to their own soul at moments of conversion or inner deepening of the life of grace.

Then Jesus puts before her his great revelation: " *'I who am speaking to you, said Jesus, 'I am he.'* " It is as if he is saying to the woman, "*You are waiting for the Messiah. But the Messiah is I who am talking to you now at this very moment. Do not expect another. It is truly me, me alone. You expect that he will teach you all things. Therefore, listen to me, surrender to my word, believe deeply what I am saying.*"

How striking: the Lord meets a lost, somewhat dejected woman in the midst of doing a simple daily chore, getting water at the well; he tells this woman personally more than he has told other important people in Israel. Jesus takes her into his deepest confidence and gives her in his own words the great tidings Israel had waited for so desperately. The woman had led a kind of checkered life, yet he selects her among countless others to receive his most sublime communication.

We see the same thing happening over and over again in the Gospels. The public sinner, the tax collector, the public woman Mary Magdalene, the criminal dying next to Jesus on the cross and here the Samaritan woman—all receive a self revelation of Jesus that many other righteous men and women did not receive. The reason for this loving self communication of our Lord cannot be because they were more sinful than others but because they were more humbly aware of their sinfulness. They felt their inner poverty, their desperate need to be uplifted by some Love that transcended them infinitely. Their sins were too glaring, too public, too obvious to themselves and others to be rationalized away.

Of course, all people, we included, are sinners. But if our sins are not too obvious we are inclined to feel so much better than we truly are. We feel safe and secure in our secret arrogance. We do not feel much of the ego desperation we all need to experience if we really want to surrender to the Lord. Ego desperation means that we have found out that we cannot save ourselves, that our clever projects are not sufficient by themselves alone to justify us in the eyes of God, no matter how punctual and precise we are in the fulfillment of our religious duties. The Lord can only enter into hearts that are empty of feelings of self sufficiency. To become worshipers in spirit and truth, to recognize the savior as the woman did, we must allow the Spirit to invade our hearts.

His telling her that he is the Messiah is the greatest surprise in her life. His answer is the solution to all the problems that have arisen in her heart. Elsewhere (Mt. 11:25-26) Jesus had said that it pleased the Father to hide this great truth from the wise and learned but to reveal it to the simple. It is good also to remember that Jesus performed no miracles in Samaria. This withholding of extraordinary deeds of power would underline the more spiritual nature of his mission, which he revealed in this one incident. Of course, Jesus knew all along that he was the Messiah.

If he would have announced it too openly among the Jewish people, his message might have evoked all kinds of political expectations and movements. The true nature of his divine message would have been confused and obscured. There was less danger of this happening in a country district like Samaria in a discussion with an obscure woman about worship. To her Jesus reveals without any reticence what he had communicated to no one else. For her this revelation marks the climax of her surprising conversation with this stranger.

It is almost impossible for us to grasp how fantastic this moment really is. Here is a sinful simple woman before whom God stands incarnated in Christ. However, we know in faith that this miracle of divine self disclosure happens over and over again. She heard only that he was the expected Messiah. If the miracle repeats itself in our lives, we hear immensely more. The Risen Lord may touch us at times and we may hear his overwhelming words: *"I who am speaking to you, I am he."* And we know he is our Lord and God, our Redeemer.

"At this point his disciples returned, and were surprised to find him speaking to a woman, though none of them asked, 'What do you want from her?' or 'Why are you talking to her?' " (Jn. 4:27-28).

The rest of the story tells us about how this conversation affected other people. We hear first the surprise of the disciples who returned from buying food just as Jesus had made the astonishing announcement that overwhelmed her. They were very

surprised, almost taken aback, that Jesus would be in
deep and serious conversation with a woman. No
Rabbi who respected himself would ever have done so.
The Rabbis of that time looked on woman as inferior
to man. An ancient prayer often used was: "Blessed
are thou, O Lord . . . who has not made me a
woman." But the disciples had become wise enough
not to question him about his unorthodox com-
portment. By now they had learned that there were
always deeper reasons behind Jesus' straying from the
conventions of the Rabbis.

Note that the disciples returned "at this point."
Divine providence had arranged things in such a way
that they did not return earlier. In that case they
would have interrupted the conversation that would
climax in Jesus' self-revelation. And yet they came
back just in time to witness how the Lord broke with
all convention and pointedly stretched his mission out
to women, a thing unheard of at that time. They will
discover a few moments later how he even made her
his first missionary among the Samaritan people. He
gave them a lesson in the emancipation of woman.

Not only in Judaism of that day but in nearly all
religions before Christ the woman as woman received
small regard, though some exceptional women would
be highly admired. Christ's appreciation of woman is
outstanding in a period in which Greek and Roman
thinkers debated in the schools whether woman had a
soul or not. His admiration for her was so extraordinary that even his followers found it difficult
for centuries to live up to the height of his respect for

her. It was the Lord Jesus who stressed the worth of woman as equal with man; he gave her her chance; he saw her possibilities, and, consequently, he has been repaid by Christian women all over the world and through the centuries with a loyalty of devotion that has been astounding.

In the midst of daily chores
You struck her tired heart
With faith and holy expectation.
She was a simple woman
Small and forlorn on a country road
Yet you kindled in her, as in few others,
The yearning for the promised One,
The Anointed of God,
Who would mellow harsh humanity,
Gentling it like aromatic oil.
You gave her these new and marvelous tidings
Because she acknowledged her poverty of soul
Her need to be uplifted by your Love.
Arrogance died quickly in her.
Lord, I too feel small and forlorn
On the country road of an empty life.
Please, strike my tired heart,
Anoint me with your holy oil
So that my stubborn life may soften
And be permeated by your life, my Lord.

THE MISSION OF THE CHRISTIAN
IN THE WORLD

The woman put down her water jar and hurried back to the town to tell the people, "Come and see who has told me everything I ever did; I wonder if he is the Christ?" This brought people out of the town and they started walking toward him (Jn. 4:28-30).

The woman quickly left when the disciples arrived. God, in his loving direction of all events, had things arranged in such a way that she received the surprising message of Jesus before being disturbed by the arrival of so many Jewish strangers. She forgets to take her filled water jar along. She does not even think about giving Jesus the drink he had asked her for. She is so touched by his words and his presence that she forgets all else and hurries back to tell the people she meets about what has happened to her. To be as fast as possible, she does not want to be encumbered by a jar full of water on her head. She is aware that her simple excited words can never communicate what it means to meet Jesus. Therefore, she says, "Come and see."

The real messenger of the Lord never trusts his

human power of persuasion. His only hope is to get the people to look for themselves, to expose themselves to the miracle of a divine or prophetic presence, to see with the eyes of faith, hope and love. To be able to move people to come and see, the messenger himself must be a person who truly came and saw. When others sense what "coming and seeing" has done to him, they begin to wonder: "Maybe there is something to it?" The grace that touched the messenger begins already to touch them, readying them to come and see. The experience of the Divine cannot lie buried in our hearts. It cries out in us to be communicated to our fellow men. As the psalmist sings: "I believed, and therefore I speak." (Ps. 116:10)

This is what happened to the woman at the well. She describes Jesus as "a man who has told me everything I ever did." John often uses the word man, *anthropos,* when referring to Jesus. He wants to emphasize his real humanity. The whole story of the Samaritan woman stresses this humanity. Jesus is not some ghostlike appearance, but really a human being, a person tired, thirsty, really one of us.

She told the people that he told her everything she ever did. She had been so surprised by Jesus' knowledge of her entire life since her first marriage that she blurts out to everyone she meets: he has told me everything I ever did. The people must have asked her what then did he tell her. When she told them, they must have been astounded. They knew only too well her past and present life; that a Jewish stranger just passing by knew the same without being told must have made them curious.

The woman leaves it up to the people to draw their own conclusions when they meet with our Lord. She puts her thoughts into a question: "I wonder if he is the Christ?" In her own heart she is already convinced that this gentle stranger, with his powerful presence, is indeed the Messiah. She believes her own graced experience but senses that she cannot really give to others what was given to her in a direct encounter with the Lord. Therefore, she puts her question in such a way that people have to come and see and arrive at their own response in faith and love when touched by the grace of Jesus. Her way is wise. By avoiding the impression of any imposition of her own opinion or experience, she does not evoke resistance or contradiction. If anything she raises interest and curiosity in the people. Her excitement, her witnessing for an experience that visibly has moved her, the questions she evoked in their hearts had a good effect. *"This brought people out of the town and they started walking toward him."*

The people rushed off immediately. John pictures them on the way, the curious crowd gripped by a mysterious expectation. The disciples had just arrived from the same town. They brought back some loaves. The Samaritan woman brought back some people. It is the Lord who determines who will be his messenger among men. It may be a disciple who lived with him for a long time; it may be a sinner just converted. Here we see what the words of our Lord can do. The woman, sinful, lost and unhappy, becomes at once his messenger announcing the Good News to anyone she meets.

Abandoning her water jar is a symbol of her readiness to abandon anything that would interfere with the call she experiences, the call to go out and bring people to Jesus that they may come and see for themselves. How often this miracle of the call would repeat itself in countless people after her, how they too would abandon things to dedicate themselves to the message of the Lord. God had filled her with charity, moving her to let other people share in her happiness. Earthly treasures we may want to keep for ourselves; the treasures of grace we should always want to share. What is touching in the faith of the woman is that she cannot imagine that people would not surrender to the divine attraction and the gentle grace of the presence and the words of Jesus.

Meanwhile, the disciples were urging him, "Rabbi, do have something to eat"; but he said, "I have food to eat that you do not know about." So the disciples asked one another, "Has someone been bringing him food?" But Jesus said: "My food is to do the will of the one who sent me, and to complete his work" (Jn. 4:31-34).

The disciples urge Jesus to eat some of the food they had brought. They call him Rabbi. Their gentle urging is respectful and without familiarity. They never called him brother while Jesus himself called them sometimes "My brethren." They felt it was time to eat after the long journey they had made together and they realized that Jesus, like they themselves, must be hungry by now. Jesus, their spiritual teacher, sees this as an occasion to teach them something about what should come first in life and how the joy of the saving task can make us delay other things to be taken care of. We see here how Jesus really puts himself into his work. He did it with his whole heart and soul. He is so taken up in his task that he excludes other things for the moment. Teaching and gracing the lonely woman fills him with joy and delight; it was like food and drink to him; it makes him momentarily forget his weariness, thirst and hunger. He feels even more exalted now that he sees others coming with her to whom he may communicate his message of love and salvation.

Because the disciples were not there when Jesus was able to open the woman up to grace, they could not know the nourishment of heart and spirit Jesus had enjoyed. He said to them therefore: "I have food to eat that you do not know about." In Verse 34, Jesus himself explains what kind of food he means. It is spiritual nourishment. As so often in this Gospel, the disciples misunderstand their spiritual teacher by taking his words literally. They ask each other: "Has someone been bringing him food?" They wonder, for they did not expect that a Samaritan would have brought food to Jesus, a Jewish stranger. They had left him thirsty and hungry and now they found him refreshed and he did not want to eat anything. Had he not sent them out to buy food? Perhaps this woman had given Jesus something to eat? Yet they are too respectful to question Jesus himself; they talk only among each other about what might have happened. Jesus went quietly on to explain what he meant.

"My food is to do the will of the one who sent me, and to complete his work."

What strikes us is the generosity with which the Lord used his life. His days, as narrated in the Gospels, were filled with endless appeals. And always the Lord went without waiting. "Let us go at once," he would say. Often the disciples were upset and concerned. They felt that he was wearing himself out. The crowds would besiege him at times and he would spend himself eagerly to meet their needs. The Lord teaches us and his disciples that we Christians too do have to live out in Jesus the will of the Father who sent us into this world; that we too have to join him in completing the mysterious work of the Father, that our generous participation in this completion of creation should be the nourishment of our spiritual life as it was for Jesus. But we are grudging and niggardly with our energies and our time. We reserve much for our own pleasure and relaxation and dole out small bits of our energy to the task God gave us to do. We are not really there and as a result many jobs are poorly done and the completion of creation is badly served. We toss in a little of our attention and tell people how tired we already are and how we need to go slowly and not overdo things.

To be allowed to do God's will as well as he could was the whole meaning of life for Christ. A Christian is a person who has been touched by this spirit of the

Lord and is growing up in his likeness. He tries to discover his own unique mission in life, his irreplaceable contribution to the kingdom, to the completion of the work of the Father.

The "my" in "my food" is emphatic. Whatever others may feel about the meaning of life, for Jesus the very food of life is to do the divine will. Obedience to the divine will is his major concern. Singlemindedly he presses on. The mission of Jesus is to finish the work the Father sent him to do. Later, at the Last Supper, he will pray: "I have completed the work you gave me to do." (Jn. 17:4) And in John 19:28 and 30, Jesus, knowing that all things are now completed, said, "It is accomplished."

The will and the work of the Father were completed when Jesus died on the cross. Yet in another sense, the full completion of the loving work of the Father in this world demands our participation in Jesus' obedience in our daily life. Our mind and heart, our will and love, like those of Jesus, must be taken up with the will of the Father and his work so completely that they actually become the food of our spiritual life. Completing his task is a necessity for Jesus, something he needs to do to go on, to live. Because of our sinfulness and inertia, our resistance and rebellion, we may often sabotage the work the Father gives us to do in this world. Even if we are faithful to the unique direction the Father gives to our life, our faithfulness will always be imperfect. At any moment we may betray our mission, leave the work undone, get sidetracked by interests that estrange us from our task. Jesus could never do that. While we try to follow Jesus in his fidelity to his Father's work, we will never make it as perfectly our continuous nourishment as Jesus did.

It may be helpful for our spiritual life to realize that three expressions in this verse highlight three of the leading themes of the Gospel of St. John. "To do the will of the Father" is also spoken about in other places (cf. 5:30; 6:28; 14:31). It reminds us of the words used in St. Paul's Epistle to the Hebrews (10:6-10). St. Paul cites there Ps. 40 to explain that the sacrifice of Christ is not like the sacrifices of the Old Testament, that his true sacrifice is to do the will of God. The same is true of the followers of Christ.

"Of the one who sent me," is an expression used by Jesus twenty-five times in this Gospel. John wants to stress the sending of the Logos in the world by the Father. It helps us to see our own life as a being sent into the world with Jesus to live out a unique life direction.

"To complete his work" is also found in many other places (cf. 5:36; 9:4; 17:4; 19:28). The culmination of this directive of Jesus' life is found in the cry from the cross, "It is accomplished."

These three themes of doing the divine will, of being faithful to a unique divine mission, of completing with Jesus the work of the Father in this world should be the leading themes of a true Christian life. The central place they occupy in St. John's Gospel demonstrates again how much his writings can be used as guidelines for a spiritual life in Christ.

May I forget my water jar
And everything that weighs me down.
May I rise unencumbered in the sky
Like a carefree bird
Singing: Come and see
How the Lord has set me free,
How all creation is a melody,
A song for God,
A song still open ended,
An unfinished symphony.
May I complete a little
The mysterious work of the Father
On planet earth
In my small corner of history.
May I share the divine completion of creation.
Let it be for me the very fact of life,
My daily nourishment.
Let me spend myself eagerly
As Jesus did.

MINISTRY AND SPIRITUALITY

When the woman had left and the disciples asked him to eat, Jesus reminded them of the work he had to complete in this world. His gracious conversation with the woman at the well had been part of this ministry. Now the people of Sychar are approaching, and with them, another invitation to complete his divine mission. Jesus witnesses for the urgency of his ministry: *"Have you not a saying: Four months and the harvest? Well, I tell you: Look around you, look at the fields; already they are white, ready for harvest!"* (Jn. 4:35).

He had compared his ministry, his doing of the Father's will, with daily nourishment. Now he switches from the image of food to that of harvest. Between Jacob's well where he stood and Sychar from which the people were drawing near him, the fields had been planted in wheat and barley, covering the earth with a thrifty growth of green. Jesus refers to the saying that it will still be four months before the harvest. He contrasts this necessary delay in reaping with a spiritual harvest that may happen here at this moment. The harvest of the earth is still months off, but the fields of the spirit are white for harvest, ready to be cut. "Look around you, look at the field." There on the path through the young grain, the Samaritans are coming in their white garments shining in the sun. They were the grain Jesus saw, white for harvest, ready to be gathered into the divine granary.

He speaks about two kinds of harvest just as he spoke about two kinds of food. He makes both food and harvest symbols of the spiritual realm that is more fundamental and vital for our lives than the material appearances pointing to it. We may be as blind to this realm as the disciples at times appeared to be. We may be unduly impressed by the wealth, status, learning, talents, charm or power of the people we meet. Rarely do we think about the unique graced calling and dignity bestowed on each of them. We seldom ask ourselves how we may facilitate their fidelity to this hidden treasure that is infinitely more worthwhile than their mundane appearance and success. Or we may unwittingly look with condescension on a poor man, an old sick woman, a retarded child, an outcast, a foreigner who has difficulty in adapting himself smoothly to our ways. Again we do not see in faith that each of these persons too is blessed with a unique dignity and calling. When we look with the eyes of the Lord, people become precious; for each of them is called to play a unique role in his kingdom.

In his outcry that the fields are ready for the harvest, we sense the urgency he felt about his ministry. Inspired by his Spirit, we should share in his urgent sense of mission. When seed has been planted in the earth, there is no way of getting around the waiting time. But in the realm of the Spirit some fields may be ready for harvest; some people may be primed by grace for a new awakening at the occasion of our word or example, of our kindness and consideration.

We may believe in advance that the average person who is not Christian has no receptivity for the message of the Lord. He may not be ready but then again he may. We do not know what God has done in the secret of his heart. Similarly we assume easily that the average Christian is not yet available for the invitation to a deeper spiritual life. But how do we know? If we do not give others a chance to hear the whisper of the Spirit, those who may be longing for a deeper life in Jesus may never reach the divine intimacy they were invited to. At the right moment we failed to be God's instrument for them. Our life is short and the task is great; too often we stand idle in the vineyard forgetting that our mission is urgent. We are reminded of Matthew's words: "The harvest is rich but the laborers are few, so ask the Lord of the harvest to send laborers to his harvest" (Mt. 9:37-38).

" . . . already they are white, ready for harvest!" This exclamation of Jesus shows us the amazing hope and trust that animated him. We hear the same enthusiasm at other moments of his life. A few Greeks ask to see him and Jesus dreams of a golden harvest all over the world. Seventy disciples sent out by him to preach the good news return excited over the things that had happened. How little it was in comparison with the gigantic task to be fulfilled during millennia to come, yet Jesus exults: "I watched Satan fall like lightning from heaven." (Lk. 10:18) A criminal dying next to him on the cross cried out to him and he assured him paradise. He himself died with a shout of triumphant hope: "It is accomplished" (Jn. 19:30). And here, in his meeting with the woman at the well and her countrymen, he sparkles with the same amazing hope. A hesitant woman whose life has been confused and is in many ways a failure shows some faith in him and gets the people she meets to come and see for themselves. As he sees them walking toward him he exalts about whole fields that are white, ready for the harvest.

Any small sign of God's influence on people was for him a symbol of the miracles of grace to be hoped for. His is a divine hope we too should carry in our hearts no matter how small the impact of our life and love seems to be. We have so little trust in the power of grace. We look around us and say, shaking our heads, there is still much time before the harvest. The corn is still green. We should wait until it is ready for the sickle. We despair too easily and feel that the time for spiritual awakening is not near. We neglect to put ourselves in touch with the treasures of truth and the mysteries of grace found in Christ. Within this kingdom of grace, we will be purified. The golden corn of our unique life call in Christ will be separated from the straw of worldly attachment so that we may grow daily in fidelity to our destiny.

"Already the reaper is being paid his wages, already he is bringing in the grain for eternal life, and thus

sower and reaper rejoice together. For there the proverb holds good: one sows, another reaps; I sent you to reap a harvest you had not worked for. Others worked for it; and you have come into the rewards of their trouble" (Jn. 4:36-38).

How alive and all embracing the imaginative thought of Jesus is. First he thinks about the harvest, making it a symbol of people to be gathered in the one Spirit like golden grain in the granary; now his creative imagination calls up the image of the reaper; then it goes back to the sowers and turns to the disciples personally. He speaks first about the wages of the reaper. He explains that the wages are the very bringing in of the grain for eternal life. Eternal life is the present gift of the life of the Spirit reaching into everlasting life with God. But how can we experience our spreading of the spiritual life in and with Jesus as "wages"? Jesus himself clarifies that for us in what follows: "and thus sower and reaper rejoice together."

Rejoicing—that is the remuneration given to us by the Spirit when we see in faith the fruits gathered by our graced presence to others. This rejoicing will reach its fullness in the hereafter; it will fill our eternity, outshining the vanity of earthly rewards. Already here we may know moments of spiritual joy, divine announcements of the life of joy to be ours in eternity because of God and his grace illuminating redeemed humanity. This joy is most holy and pure, unblemished by our selfishness. For it is a joy inspired by God's unfolding presence in the persons we have been called to care for spiritually. God's goodness to them and us is the only source of this pure joy in Jesus.

Jesus assures us that this joy will be given to both the sower and the reaper. This reward is different from that received by a farmer on earth. He may sow a field of wheat and not live to enjoy the harvest and the wages brought by it. In the life of the Spirit this cannot be the case. The joy of the harvest will come to the sower as well as to the reaper. The reaper is bound to the sower by the unity of the divine enterprise; he is simply completing in Jesus, what the other commenced in Jesus. Therefore, the two rejoice together in the Lord. In the kingdom of grace there is no separation between sowing and reaping. The prophecy of Amos has come true: *"The days are coming now— it is Yahweh who speaks—when harvest will follow directly after plowing, the treading of grapes soon after sowing, when the mountains will run with new wine and the hills all flow with it"* (Amos 9:13). In faith sower and reaper stand together in the eternal "now" of the eschatological harvest; they share joy in the Spirit over the work of grace they are called to participate in.

Jesus encourages the sowers among us to keep their eyes of faith on the eschatological harvest they cannot yet see with their earthly eyes. The fields may look barren, the life of the Spirit neglected, spiritual teachers unpopular and ludicrous, pushed aside as dreamers who delay the progress of science, technology and humanity. The sowers of the Divine may live in a dry period of the history of salvation in which they can only plod up and down the furrows under the bleakness of overcast skies. They sow patiently in the spring, steadily teaching the good tidings, being present in love and gentleness though not even one blade may show through. Their work is unnoticed, without struggle, passion or tragedy, without triumph or the grandeur of conspicuous heroism. The pain of the hidden life of a sower may take place in his study behind his typewriter, or at home with his unwilling children, or in the classroom with his resistant students.

If I am called uniquely by the Lord to the quiet undramatic work of the sower as a writer or painter, composer or teacher, father or mother, who has to bring a spiritual message contemporaries are no longer longing for, let me be faithful to my humble calling, believing in the Lord that the bitter task he calls me to in the winter of unbelief will not be in vain. He will call others to gather the harvest from what I have sown. And I will enjoy this harvest with the reapers as my own in Christ.

Perhaps I am called to live in a period or place in the history of salvation in which gloom and dejection are less present, in which Christianity is no longer a melancholy fading enterprise. It is the period of the reaper. I should rejoice about the harvest which was denied to so many who were faithful witnesses before me. I get the credit; they got the pain. I should humbly admit that the faith and courage of the sowers were probably greater than mine, for they had to work without seeing any sign of the harvest to come. They kept alive the stream of love and truth in the caverns of the human heart. They made it possible for this hidden water to periodically well up abundantly in the midst of Christianity. I profit from their labor and suffering.

Ultimately it is the Incarnate Word who is the sower, who merits and plants the seed of grace in humanity. The Holy Spirit is the reaper who has to achieve the sanctification of humanity and history. Sowers and reapers in the history of Christian spirituality are instruments of the Word and the Spirit. The Divine Sower, the Divine Reaper, are their light and strength, the power of all their words. It is Jesus and his Spirit who touch people, who draw them. Our Lord merited the coming of the Holy Spirit and sent him; it is the Divine Spirit who completes his mission and who is the true Reaper. When we have all done what we could to be sowers and reapers in the Lord, we can only say that we are useless servants.

Dignity you bestowed abundantly
On every human being.
Each one is a sanctuary
Hiding the mystery of a mission
That outshines in the eyes of angels
Mundane appearance and success.
It may be a retarded child,
A sick old woman, an outcast of society,
A foreigner who talks haltingly,
Each one is splendid as a lustrous opal,
Precious as gold in the sight of God.
Each one is redeemed by the blood of Jesus
And called by the Spirit
To play a role in the Kingdom
As will be known hereafter
When veils fall away
And the mystery of each man
Will be revealed.
May I sing to people
About the mystery they deeply are,
About the Spirit in their plodding lives.
Already the fields are white
Ready for the harvest.
But few are the laborers
To gather your chosen ones
In the granary of the Spirit,
To separate the golden grain
Of their graced destiny
From the straw of attachment.
Lord, send me out into the fields
And when I have done all I could
Remind me kindly that I was only
A useless servant.

THE GIFT OF FAITH

"Many Samaritans of that town had believed in him on the strength of the woman's testimony when she said, 'He told me all I have ever done', so when the Samaritans came up to him, they begged him to stay with them" (Jn. 4: 39-40).

Jesus' meeting with the woman ends in a striking finale. The touching climax will be the Samaritan believers claiming Jesus as "The savior of the world."

This lovely ending begins with the witness of the woman. She had been impressed by Jesus' knowledge of her life: "He told me all I have ever done." She had been more impressed by his person. The grace that went out from him had touched her inmost being. It must have shone forth in her eyes, the tone of her voice, the radiance of her face. Many Samaritans were moved by the grace of Jesus she carried in her changed appearance, in her soft and eager words. They went to him readied for his grace. When they reached him they were overcome by his presence; they begged him to stay with them. Our Lord was moved by their simple faith. The sensitive Jesus must have been filled to the brim with joy and wonder. They came to him already believing! He had travelled laboriously through Judea and Galilee, bringing his word and his grace but few had followed him. He had performed many miracles yet found few who surrendered to his love and truth. Nicodemus, a pious and learned Scribe, came to the faith slowly and hesitantly. Inner conceit is an obstacle to grace. Conceit may be veiled and hidden. The light of the Lord cannot reach the hearts of men who feel important and impressive. A subtle arrogance poisons their soul. The Samaritans had little reason for arrogance. They were a despised minority in Israel, considered as loathsome as the heathens. Their pride may have been broken by their painful history. Faith found a steady entrance into their mellowed hearts. Far from looking down on him, they begged him to stay. The men and women of Jerusalem did not insist that Jesus stay with them. Afterwards he visits Jericho; not one person asked him to remain another day.

The Samaritans who came to him had believed in him because of the woman's witness. They were struck by the grace of Jesus she carried with her as a silent power of holy radiance. We should not dismiss their conversion as naive credulity. Jesus may give his grace through anyone he chooses. He may make any person the minister of his message for a shorter or longer duration—sometimes for a lifetime, in other cases only for a crucial moment in the life of one fellow man.

It is not the personal charm or excellence, repute or learning of the messenger that leads to conversion.

The merits of the messenger may distract attention away from the message; the bearer of the good tidings may stand too much in their way. By contrast, the simplicity, the vulnerability of a messenger, may highlight how immeasurably beyond him the mystery of the message is he is called to proclaim. It becomes almost impossible to confuse him and his message. We no longer mistake the medium for the message.

Many people of Sychar were able to go beyond their feelings about the woman of ill repute; they sensed the power that had touched her. We often have to do the same. For we all are dependent on others for the widening of our vision of faith. And these others sent by the Lord are by no means always saints. Centuries of bitter church criticism have made us oversensitive to the sins and limitations of all Christians, especially of those whom God sent us as his representatives. Yet, we need them like the Samaritans needed the woman of ill repute to receive the message of the Lord. Without them we would be thrown back upon our own meager resources, upon our own pious thought and feeling. How thin our image of Jesus and his truth would be without the teachings of the Church and its specialists. Christians over the ages won for us slowly and painfully—often in a bitter battle of words and wit—the treasures of insight that are ours today.

Among these feuding Christians have been scandalous people like the woman at the well. Yet they were among those chosen by Jesus to bestow on us over the ages the gift of an enlarged vision of faith. The faith vision can never be the result of my own effort alone. It is largely the gift of others whom the Spirit made channels of his light in spite of their sinfulness. When I focus too much on the imperfection of God's messengers, I may miss the message. I may fall victim to the fiction that I can broaden my faith vision sufficiently by means of my own little isolated mind. This fiction would blind me also to the enlightenment that may come to me through common people I meet in everyday life. Everyone of them may be chosen by the Lord to be his messenger. I myself, no matter my poverty, may be called upon by the Lord to be his messenger to a soul in distress. I must not be so overcome by the awareness of my sinfulness that I begin to doubt that Jesus can ever use me for his kingdom. He can use me and he wants to. I should never refuse his invitation.

I may be used by grace to bring people to the Lord, not to myself. I should feel that grace really succeeded if those who come to me end up begging the Lord himself to abide with them. My only desire should be that they long no longer for me but for Jesus.

He stayed for two days, and when he spoke to them many more came to believe; and they said to the woman, "Now we no longer believe because of what you told us; we have heard him ourselves and we know that he really is the savior of the world" [Jn. 4:41-42].

In the Book of Revelation our Lord says: "Behold I stand at the door and knock" (Rev. 3:20). Jesus does not wait until we knock at his door. He knocks at the door of our heart and blessed is he who opens to him.

The venerable Francis Libermann says, "The Divine Master then enters; he eats with him the bread of sorrow and troubles of this world and makes him also eat with Him the bread of His love, of joy and strength." That is what happened to the Samaritans. They had lived in darkness. The Savior came to knock at their door. He used the woman at the well to make them hear his voice. The Samaritans were faithful to that first grace. In their longing to see and hear him who was knocking, they opened their door with joy and eagerness. They went to him in humble anticipation; they asked him over and over again to stay with them. And the Divine Master shared their life for two days.

How precious the graces our Lord must have poured out during that time. The word of Jesus is so potent that no person who is well disposed can resist its gentle power. Where the word of Jesus meets a humble heart, its impact is astounding.

The words of Jesus have not lost their potency. If we use not our own words but allow him to speak through us, we may witness the same miracle in listeners of good will, ready to surrender to any grace that comes their way. But it is not easy to speak the pure words of Jesus. We are inclined to say a lot of things that please our vanity, show our cleverness, and bind the admiration of people to us and not to him. It takes a lifetime to purify our speech from selfishness, to allow him alone to be present in our language of faith.

The Samaritans believed in Jesus not because of miracles; he did not do any in that town. They believed *"because we have heard him ourselves."* It was the power of his word that made them believe. The faith engendered by his word was much more penetrating and luminous than the initial faith evoked by the story they had heard about the miraculous insight of Jesus in the life of the woman. That is why they said to that woman: "Now we no longer believe because of what you told us. The faith given to us by your word has deepened immensely because we ourselves have heard his divine teaching; we ourselves have experienced his presence. His word has filled us with joy and hope. Now we know for certain that he really is the savior of the world."

The woman had introduced them to Jesus, but belief in Jesus is not true faith as long as it rests on the hearing alone. True faith presupposes a personal encounter with Christ. The enlightenment of mind we acquire as a result of the word and example of our parents, of our priests in the parish and teachers in school is important; it is a gift of the Lord who reaches us through them. It may open up our intellect, our understanding, which is an opening to true faith, but faith itself happens when we encounter Christ and personally surrender. Teachings can expand and refine the vision of faith, our understanding of its content. Therefore, the cultivation of our vision of faith by learning should never stop. This knowledge, however, should be continually transformed into a personal faith by loving encounter with Christ in scripture and sacraments and in our heart. This faith nourished by our personal presence to the Lord of life is true faith.

The Samaritans, after receiving a first enlightenment by listening to the woman, now received the grace of true faith in encountering Jesus himself. We are not less well off than the Samaritans. Jesus is with us today in his grace, in his word, in his Church and sacraments. When we meet him in prayerful recollection we can hear him personally as if we sat among the listeners at Sychar. We can be present to the risen Lord every day, not only for two days. What he told them during his stay, they had to remember for a lifetime. We have available to us at any moment of our lives the inspired word of Jesus in the Gospel and in his Church. What ultimately counts is not the hearing, no matter how necessary, but the surrender in and through grace even if we don't hear anything anymore for a long time because the Lord allows us to dwell in darkness.

The Samaritans confessed their faith in the words *"we know that he really is the savior of the world."* It has now become a faith of personal recognition, the graced knowledge which a person only receives when he himself drinks the living water. Such faith cannot easily be shaken by fads and fancies or by false reasonings of a mere secular science. The true believer deeply "knows." Only prayerful encounter with Jesus and his word can ready us for the grace of this lived knowledge of faith.

The Samaritans profess that they "know" him as

"the savior of the world." The word savior implies an experience of deliverance, of a saving from blindness, evil and despair. Jesus is more than the flawless model of our life. Flawless models are frustrating when we are unable to live up to them. But Jesus is more than our model. He really saves. He rescues us from sin, despair and limitations, lifting us up to divine heights, making us share in the life of the Holy Trinity itself. He is not only our savior but of all people. Therefore, the Samaritans call Him the savior of the world. The conversion of the Samaritans is the first sign that all—not only Jewish people—are called to be saved by our Lord.

How strikingly the growth in faith is expressed in this story. Jesus is first seen as a mere Jew, resting at the well, then as a prophet, next as Messiah, and finally as Savior of the world. With the Samaritan woman, with the men and women of Sychar, we kneel down in loving adoration, silently repeating with them: "You really are the savior of the world."

You stand at the door
And knock, my Lord
Until I open up.
You want to eat with me
The bread of daily sorrow
And to break for me
The bread of your eternal love.
Let me open up with joy and eagerness
To receive you as my savior,
The savior of the world.
Let me recognize your knocking
When it comes through someone else
No matter how simple or sinful he may be.
Let me see beyond his charm or rudeness
The Spirit who may have chosen him
To light a candle in my life.
Every man I meet may carry
A message of the Paraclete for me.
He may be called
To mold and fashion me
In the image of my Lord.
Let me never doubt
That the same spirit may use me too,
In spite of my own sinfulness,
To bring some love and light
To fellow sinners I may meet
More intimately.

EPILOGUE

FORMATIVE SCRIPTURE READING

FORMATIVE SCRIPTURE READING

This meditative reading of the narrative of Jesus' meeting the woman at the well could be seen as an example of formative scripture reading.

The kind of reading most familiar to us is that by which we gather information. We have been trained in how to do such reading from early life. Without this gathering of useful information, we would not be able to function well in daily surroundings. The media aim mainly at giving us information. So do our schools, our government, state and city agencies. No wonder that it is difficult to shift from this type of attention to a different one that benefits mainly our inner formation. The gathering of information by informative reading has its right place and time; it guides our life in relation to the people and institutions we have to interact with effectively. In relation to scripture, informative reading is necessary too; it makes us familiar with the basic structure and meaning of its contents. Helpful also is informative reading *about* scripture; it informs us about the doctrinal, theological and exegetical aspects of the sacred text. This knowledge cautions us against erroneous interpretations.

Different from the informative is the formative approach to scripture; it is meant to enlighten our unique inner formation in Christ. Our inner life can be nourished and directed in its graced uniqueness by an abiding, meditative style of scripture reading. As St. Paul says: "You must keep to what you have been taught and know to be true; remember who your teachers were, and how, ever since you were a child, you have known the holy scriptures—from these you can learn the wisdom that leads to salvation through faith in Christ Jesus. All scripture is inspired by God and can profitably be used for teaching, for refuting error, for guiding people's lives and teaching them to be holy. This is how the man who is dedicated to God becomes fully equipped and ready for any good work" (2 Tim. 3, 14-17).

The information contained in the literal text of scripture and in books about scripture cannot in and by itself guide our lives and transform us inwardly, making us holy. What makes us better equipped and ready for any good work is the unspoken mystery, the secret wisdom, and especially the personal relevance hidden under the informative layers of the text. To unearth this hidden treasure and its manifold meanings for our transformation in the Lord, we have to abide by these words, to ponder them in our hearts, to taste them.

Scripture and Self Formation

I must learn to read the scripture text as if it were written for me alone. I should try to come to an inner dialogue with the Spirit speaking in the text, hoping to find the self formation I am seeking. I do not, then, confine the Spirit speaking to me to my narrow vision; rather I allow the vision of the Spirit for my life to unfold itself so that I may be captured by it and gain new perspectives. If my vision is thus widened by the wisdom of the scriptures, I may discover more deeply the self I am before God.

To find self formation by means of scripture reading, I must be open in docility to what its text may eventually tell me about myself; I must abide with formative reading until it yields to me its treasure. Formative reading implies, moreover, my willingness to change my current self in light of the formative insight scripture may radiate to me. The word as formative has the power to transform me. It can give rise to a new self in Christ, permeating all dimensions of my life. The word as formative can lift me beyond the stirrings of my ego and vital life so that I may discover my graced life form in the Eternal Word.

The power of this formation does not depend on how much but on how well I read. One passage of scripture that really speaks to me, dwelt upon prayerfully, may form me more deeply than whole chapters devoured eagerly but merely in the way of information. The page that resonates to me formatively may be of such profundity for me at this moment of my life that I keep receiving light and inner formation in Christ every time I read it again and again.

I should not, however, expect transformation of mind and heart every time I read the scriptures

Spiritual transformation is a grace given by God when he deems it worthwhile for me. If it pleases him to test my faithfulness to formative scripture reading in the midst of aridity, I should not give up. I should realize that the deepest formation takes place in the hidden recesses of my soul. It is a work of the Holy Spirit that may go unnoticed for long stretches of time.

Actuality of Formative Scripture Reading

The need for such formative reading is felt increasingly in Christianity since the reawakening of a genuine interest in the spiritual life. Holy Scripture is a source of that life. Every Christian striving after the renewal of his inner life could profit immeasurably from a formative reading of scripture.

When we approach scripture in a formative way, we read it in such a manner that its words and mysteries help us to tune in to the inner life form the Lord has meant for us from eternity. Because scripture reading, done in this fashion, aids us to find and unfold the mystery of our graced life form hidden in Christ such reading is called formative and spirituality approached from this perspective is called Formative Spirituality.

The formative approach to scripture will prove to be an invaluable aid for many people who cannot personally profit from private direction or from spiritual direction-in-common as given in sermons and lectures on spirituality. Formative reading may provide them with the direction the Holy Spirit desires to grant them through the message of the scriptures.

Formative reading of scripture is thus a special kind of reading; it is guided by our graced aspiration to find words and meanings which can aid the disclosure and growth of the unique life form the Holy Spirit wants for us. This is the kind of reading that can enlighten us in darkness, deepen our dwelling in God's presence, fortify our fidelity to the life call, prompt our commitment to the divine transformation of the world, orient our whole life to intimacy with the Eternal Love that carries us. Briefly, it is the kind of reading that illumines and nourishes the life of self formation in Christ through the Holy Spirit.

At times we may feel like drowning in the demands, problems and preoccupations that beset us daily. The acceleration of change in church and society challenges us constantly. Inevitably, the pressure of adaptation to ever changing conditions tends to alienate us from what the Spirit calls us to be. Yet the Spirit in us does not cease to whisper his gentle invitation to find and follow God's direction for our life. He does not want us to forget about our divine destiny. Listening to the Spirit as he speaks to us in the scriptures may clarify the words that he speaks in our hearts.

While our duties and responsibilities may not allow us to spend many hours in scripture reading, we can at least set aside some of our time for this practice. Once we are committed and accustomed to this reading it becomes a most attractive and enlightening moment of our day; it quiets heart and mind, gentles our will and passion; it inspires and lifts up our soul; it gives rise to spontaneous prayer of the heart; it awakens graced intuitive understanding; it fosters wise reflection.

The Personal Aspect of Formative Scripture Reading

Formative reading is attentive to the personal message the inspired words may contain; it gently tries to still other considerations during the time allotted to this practice. This prayerful waiting for a personal message is sustained by the living faith that the Spirit knows the true path each reader is called to follow in his life, that the Spirit determines the time and the way in which the next step to be taken may be communicated through the text.

For example, in the story of the woman at the well we may be struck by the gentle way in which Jesus tries to make her aware of attachments that hinder the joyful unfolding of her life in the Lord. He reminds her of her five marriages and her present liaison in which she sought in vain for ultimate consolation. Reading this story may offer us a moment of grace. It may suddenly strike us that we too are spoken to by Jesus with love and compassion, that we too are gently reminded of our attachments to symbolic marriage partners we put in the way between him and us. Suddenly the story draws us in personally; it lights up our own life situation. We are taken up in the inner struggle of the woman; the words of Jesus about her attachments become addressed to us here and now: to become at one with him we must spot and transcend our inordinate liaisons with this world. The kind and intensity of such attachments will be different for each individual dependent on his life situation and personal make up. Unique also will be the spontaneous prayer this passage may evoke in each of us.

This is an example of a simple text in St. John and the personal message it may contain. There are other passages, for instance in the prologue of his Gospel or in the last discourse of Jesus, that are more difficult to grasp. We may even have to do some study before we will be able to profit as fully as we can from them. Such exegetical or doctrinal study is praiseworthy as long as we do it outside the time we have reserved for meditative reading. Even then we may not understand each word and sentence fully. That should not worry us. Our first aim is to obtain edification and enlightenment for our personal life in Christ. What we do not yet understand or may never understand we pass quietly by in relaxed equanimity. Prayerfully and serenely present to the text we wait in docility for what the Spirit may tell us in those parts that we are able to understand within the limits of the grace given to each of us.

Taking Time, Dwelling Gentl

A lot of our informational reading in everyday life has to be accomplished within the shortest time possible: to get ready for an examination; to get through the newspaper before taking off for work; to answer correspondence rapidly; to survey facts before participating in a meeting; to keep up with the best sellers our friends are talking about. The style of speed reading that serves fact gathering and instant problem solving is deeply rooted in our daily life, education and culture. To shift to formative reading, slowed down and interspersed with pauses of prayerful reflection, is a major change not easily accomplished.

The tendency to get our scripture reading over and done with so that we can start the next book or the next task must be removed from our mind. Before beginning to read we must tell ourselves, "This time read with ease of mind. Dwell on the text leisurely. Muse about it. Try not to become strained, tense or willful. Live in faith and hope that scripture will speak to you in its own good time. Keep quietly open for inner hints, sudden associations, flashes of insight. Maintain the inner freedom to stop reading when a thought strikes home. Dwell on it, sitting quietly or walking up and down."

When we gently persevere in our attention, new insights may arise. When, on the contrary, we approach scripture reading with the anxious drive to do a good job, to achieve inspiration, to gather information, the Spirit may not speak to us. We must give ourselves over to the calming effect of patient surrender to God's grace. When we overcome our willful attempt to do well, to make our reading really relevant, we almost feel the tautness leaving our head, the tenseness draining from our muscles. We do not command scripture to make itself clear to us at once.

We are content to be nothing more than we can be at the moment, content to receive as much or as little light as the Spirit may grant us. There is no compulsion to be more edified, more enlightened, to receive more inspiration than may be granted to us on the occasion of this reading. Gone is the eagerness to hurry up the process of self formation. A spirit of gentleness invades our presence to the text.

Vehemence shuts out anything scripture itself may give us when patiently waited upon. We do not give the text much chance to show its hidden treasures. We run through the text without really allowing it to affect us. Scripture speaks, but we cannot hear its message because we do not approach it gently. The text contains hints and suggestions, but we as gentle receptive listeners are not there to receive them. The words are rich with meaning but not for us. Instead we gather surface information as fast as we can. No time is given to let it sink in, to make it part of ourselves, to absorb it in our lives.

In daily life one of our main concerns is to gain time—time to do things, not time to receive truths that may transform us inwardly. By contrast, gentle reading opens us to what the text may disclose to us; it allows scripture to change and affect us when such change is in tune with the life form meant for us. Such reading is a mode of letting be, combined with a patient abiding with the inspired text and with the Spirit who may speak through it to us personally. This attitude leads to peace and contentment.

In daily life we may be engaged in demanding tasks;

we may be inclined to overextend ourselves in efforts that wear us out. We may deplete ourselves in vehement strife. The success we achieve may seem meager in comparison to all we went through to make this achievement come true. We may use our life as a tool for achievement in the eyes of others. We may move through life as programmed computers lacking any sense of self direction.

No wonder it seems impossible for us to let go in reading of scripture, to allow it to be a relaxing activity, not to bring to it the same demands for accomplishment that deaden our daily life. We must establish a friendly accord between us and the text. We should not feel that we have to push ourselves into the reading or hold ourselves back. We approach the text in gentle self-possession. If we cannot feel at ease with the passage we are reading, we may quietly reflect on our resistance and its source; we may go to another passage or we can put the reading aside for another time when we can more readily give our attention to it. If the situation demands that we go on with the reading in spite of our reluctance, we gently do what cannot be delayed. We do not allow ourselves to become upset by the less perfect outcome due to the inauspiciousness of the moment. We take things in stride, never trying to force inner results.

Living in faithfulness to this practice, it gradually becomes easier for us to abide with a meaningful passage, to dwell on it, to stay attuned to its message. This newly gained ease begins to affect our whole life. It stills and quiets the greediness and aggressiveness of our ego even outside the reading hour. Our ego, thus silenced during scripture reading, allows us to center our lives more in our divine self direction. While it is good to develop a strong ego in service of the kingdom, scripture reading teaches us that it harms our at oneness with Jesus to center our lives in that ego alone. Greediness and arrogance might then not only make impossible formative reading but absorb all of our life. We would be so busy keeping our ego sublime, moralistically perfect, sane and successful that no time would be left for a gentle nursing of our soul in spiritual reading, prayer and meditative presence to the Spirit and his inspiration. Formative reading mellows the ego, not by sapping its strength but by diminishing its arrogance, its false exclusiveness, its pretense of ultimacy. Any diminishment of the ego's arrogance makes us more available to the message of the Spirit.

The Humble Search for Life Illumination

Our approach in formative reading is not that of a scholar but of a humble directee seeking the grace of light. The questions that emerge are not those of curiosity or of intellectual criticism but those of inner illumination. Is there something in this text that is meaningful to my life here and now? Do I feel resistance or resonance when reading? What is the source of these feelings? Do I dwell quietly on what the words seem to be telling me? Do I find deeper meanings when engaged in recurrent reading? Where and how does what I am reading tie in with my daily life? How can the text animate and guide my spiritual growth? Out of our remembrance of daily experience, questions and issues emerge. These may stimulate us to relate the text of scripture to the actual unfolding of our graced life form. We are not at once such humble readers. Our deeper graced selves are overlaid with sophistications and make-believe attitudes. We are often too analytical; we need to feel that we always know better than others. We must rescue our deeper graced self with its finer affinities, with the light of the Spirit at its inmost core, from our arrogant approach. We must develop a formative style of reading that allows this graced self to come to the fore, to be present in simplicity and humility to the inspired words.

From what we have said so far, it might be clear that our approach to formative reading should be relaxed, serene, prayerful, tranquil, yet diligent. In service of our spiritual self formation, we must look for passages that may evoke a resonance in our lives. If that resonance happens, we must stay with the words that were able to touch us. Even if such resonance does not take place, we must be willing to give grace a chance by patiently biding our time while being faithful to formative reading. In the Spirit's good time, the text may become an avenue to inner awakening.

A main virtue to foster during this reading is docility which could be described as an inner availability to any word of the scriptures the Spirit may use to awaken us. Docility implies a serene receptivity that quiets our aggressive mind—a prayerful openness to the mystery that may hide itself in the sacred text; it is an attitude of childlike wonder ready to be surprised by unexpected manifestations of the Divine. Each time we read in such serene receptivity scripture may yield new treasures of meaning. Repeated dwelling in this way will deepen our docility and surrender to the everlasting richness we find in the scriptures.

Patient Waiting and Listening

Reading scripture this way we should not expect sudden and striking illuminations by the Holy Spirit. Formative insight usually grows slowly in us as a fruit of faithfulness to this practice. The process may take months, even years. It is like the light of day that begins hesitantly to dawn at the end of the night and takes time to rise to fullness. Formative insight may be compared to the growth of a plant. We cannot actually see the plant grow, but it happens continually, even if we see the results only after a long span of time. The same is true in regard to the growth of inner direction through reading scripture regularly in a recollected way. Gradually the transforming power of the Spirit may make itself felt and speak in the text.

The wisdom of living that comes from formative reading is not there at once; it ripens in us like a fruit slowly ripens on a tree. The tree is in us; it is the tree of our hidden life form in Christ; its fruits are the manifestations of this divine self in our thoughts, feelings and daily actions. In the beginning this tree of true life is like a winter tree, cold and stark, without foliage, leaves, blossoms and flowers. Exposure to scripture is like exposure to the radiance of the sun. Just as the tree begins to blossom in sunlight, so does the tree of our divine life begin to blossom in our awareness and action when exposed to the light of the scriptures. After long fidelity to formative reading, we may open scripture and find the words suddenly lighting up for us with inspirational beauty. Insight in our life form in Jesus has blossomed forth in our loving attention and presence to the text. We hear with new ears. Certain texts may now strike us immediately as significant for our lives, texts that were perhaps dormant for us for many years.

The initiative for such sparkling insights rests with God alone. We cannot force or compel them; we can only bide our time and wait in loving attention. Formative directives, communicated to us through spiritual reading, are not necessarily new and bright ideas. The ideas may be familiar. What is new is that they light up for us in a personal way because of the Holy Spirit. They become alive and formative: they give new form and life to our daily existence. To keep open to this lighting up of new formative directives in scripture, we should keep ourselves in an attitude of receptivity. Receptivity means being awake and peacefully on the watch for the formative directives of the Spirit that might come to us on the occasion of scripture reading. We say "might come," for we cannot force this gift of inner direction. It could happen and we must be ready if it does.

This receptivity is preserved by a gentle fidelity to scripture reading, even if the text does not mean much to us in periods of aridity. We cannot listen if we do not grow to a certain equanimity in the face of both inspiration and desolation. Neither can we listen if we are excited, excessively worried or overly aggressive. Inner silence, recollection, and gentle living limit the obstacles to receptivity.

While we cannot force divine formation through scripture reading, we can hold ourselves in readiness; we can put ourselves at the Spirit's disposal. This readiness may foster and maintain in us a keenness of hearing. We could compare this keenness of hearing with that of a mother for her baby. Before having her baby, the mother may sleep soundly through the loudest noise, but after the baby is born he only has to rustle in his crib and the mother is awake. Her keenness grows and ripens in loving attention and presence. Her loving care permeates her senses so she hears with new ears.

When we, with God's grace, live in love for him, we too may slowly develop a new inner ear. Then, when we open scripture, certain texts may "jump out" at us immediately. We become keen of hearing to the extent that we truly give ourselves over to God in the scriptures as the mother gives herself to the baby she loves.

On the other hand, we can also refuse to give ourselves to the Spirit. We may not want to hear certain communications through his word in scripture. We escape his word by refusal to listen. Our refusal may be preceded or accompanied by an experience of reluctance and resistance while reading certain scripture texts. We should prayerfully reflect on what in us might possibly give rise to such negative feelings. Does a text weary us because it indicts attachments the Spirit wants us to overcome? Do we feel offended because the text questions some merely human aspirations we have totalized in our lives, idolizing them beyond any directives God may give us? If we have to admit this is the case, we should implore him to gradually lift us beyond such attachments, ambitions and idols. Otherwise they will keep blocking our openness to the message of the text as well as our availability to the divine formation.

There exists also something like a holy reluctance and resistance emerging from our graced spirit and the unique inspired form God wants to give to our life. The signs of this graced resistance are inner peace, equanimity, and an enduring, relaxed and quiet certainty that this personal appeal of the text does not seem to be in tune with the graced uniqueness the Spirit wants to cultivate in our lives. Sometimes it may be wise to consult a spiritual director when we are unable to dispel a mounting confusion about such feelings evoked during our scripture reading. If such consultation is not available, we should do the best we can, trusting that the Holy Spirit will sanctify the soul that honestly longs and strives to find and follow the divine direction of the scriptures.

Our unique form of graced living may be increasingly disclosed to us if we are faithful to the formative reading of scripture, devoutly, docilely and reflectively over the years. This faithfulness demands a wholehearted commitment to the graced art and discipline of formative scripture reading. We must put our whole selves into this venture, centering our lives around the word of God found in the scriptures.

The Checks of Reason and Reality

All kinds of irrational feelings and desires within us may distort the message the Spirit wants to give us through the scriptures. Our scripture reading may result then in false conclusions for our lives. Therefore, we must check out the meanings and directives gathered in our reading. At times it may be wise to submit such directives to a spiritual director or to friends or loved ones who understand as well and have our best interests at heart. The more inspired we feel about our inspirations, the more we need to check them rationally and realistically. An abundance of inspiration implies an abundant possibility of subjectivistic distortions. They may sidetrack us from our divine destiny. Even the purest inspiration coming from our scripture reading may become distorted. In that case our reading becomes deformative instead of formative.

It is for that reason that we must check our spontaneous insights later on by means of doctrine, reason and reality testing. When some time has passed, we will have gained distance from the scripture reading that moved us. Less identified with the inspirations of that reading, we can now check out reasonably how wise it would be to incorporate these inspirations in our life and how well they tie in with the divine form of our life as already known to us.

We may check out formative inspirations under the following aspects. The doctrinal: Is the formative inspiration that attracts me in tune with Church doctrine? The reasonable or sensible: Is this new formative insight compatible with what is reasonable, with common sense, with reality as we know it? The consensus aspect: Would this formative inspiration seem advisable for my life in the mind of wise, experienced and sensible Christians who effectively strive after a spiritual life and who are known to be open and deeply respectful of the unique calling of others? Would this formative insight at least not be positively rejected by them? The aspect of the divine life form: Does this new formative insight tie in with my unique graced life form as known to me from former graced experiences? The aspect of fidelity to the text: Can my discovery of that formative inspiration in the scripture text be communicated to wise and well informed Christians and make sense to them? Would they be able to see some valid relation between my ideas and the scripture text I felt I discovered this inspiration in? The community: How would this new formative insight if lived by me affect my family, my fellow workers, my parish and neighborhood? Could they have some reasonable objection to such a change in my life? The aspect of inner confirmation: Does the living of the new formative insight lead to enduring peace, equanimity and relaxed determination in the Lord? Does it facilitate my life of prayer?

We must always make room for such reasonable validation. Yet we must watch for the opposite extreme. The discovery of formative meanings and their later validation must alternate; both are necessary for the finding and unfolding of our life form in Christ. As formative readers of scripture we should not become fixated on inspiration or validation. When we stress validating only, all our scripture reading may become informational and rationalistic. For example, we may look at the scripture text only from the viewpoint of exegesis, systematic theology, history or literary criticism. These disciplines express certain meanings of the text concisely in concepts and words exactly delineated by the rational mind. This anchorage in reason and precise scholarship is praiseworthy and necessary, but the scripture reader in search of personal inspiration needs to go beyond it. He needs room to relate the scripture text to actual and possible formative insights for his own unique life, insights not yet conceptualized or exactly formulated.

Formative reading creates that room. Therefore, we should not engage in rational text critique during our formative scripture reading. We should not ask anxiously or curiously, "Does the author express himself grammatically well? What does he sound like from a literary viewpoint? How does his idea fit into a theological or philosophical vision I just read a book about? Would my sophisticated colleagues be impressed by what he is saying? Is the inspired writer saying anything new? Does the evangelist or apostle know human psychology? What would exegetes say about this text?" Such questions may be of utmost importance at other moments but at this moment of humble receptivity for the sake of formative inspiration, they should be postponed.

During scripture reading, we may be tempted to keep interrupting formative openness by shifting our attention constantly to learned footnotes at the bottom of the page. It is advisable to study these footnotes carefully but preferably at another time. Once we have a general idea of the doctrinal and exegetical meaning of the scripture passage we are reading, we should not interrupt our formative presence by returning explicitly to conceptual explanation and factual information. It is difficult to dwell prayerfully on the life message of scripture if we attempt simultaneously to scrutinize the logical, literary or ethnographical details of each sentence we are reading.

Formative Scripture Reading and Life Experience

When grace makes us proficient in formative reading of scripture, we begin spontaneously to associate fragments of scripture with fragments of experience. An example can be found in the spiritual writings of St. John of the Cross. In Book II, Chapter

6, Paragraph 5 of the *Ascent of Mount Carmel,* he writes as follows:

"That parable our Redeemer told in the eleventh chapter of St. Luke is noteworthy here (Lk. 11:5). He related that a man went to a friend at midnight to ask for three loaves (symbolizing these three virtues of faith, hope and charity). And he asserted that the man asked for them at midnight to indicate that the soul must acquire these three virtues by a darkness in its faculties regarding all things, and must perfect itself in these virtues by means of this night."

St. John associates this fragment of scripture with an experience that had been very striking to him in his own life and in the lives of some of his directees. He and they had experienced the dark night of the soul and how they needed the support of the three theological virtues, faith, hope, and charity, on their journey through this experience of loneliness and aridity. Moved by this gripping fragment of his life experience, he sees the three loaves as symbolizing these three virtues. "Midnight" in this Gospel story signifies for him in the light of the same experience the darkness that he suffered in his faculties when God allowed him to feel only emptiness and spiritual deprivation. And he explains how he experienced more than ever in this darkness the need to acquire these virtues of faith, hope and charity.

This personal experiential reading by St. John of the Cross is surely not Church doctrine but neither is it at odds with it. His formative reading is evidently not an exegetical clarification of the scripture texts. It is meant to enlighten and inspire himself and his readers in regard to the formative praxis of faith, hope and charity in the midst of the darkness of soul allowed by God as part of the emergence of the divine life form in certain people.

Take a text such as "We are to love, then, because he loved us first" (Jn. 4:19). An informative reading of this text may yield doctrinal understanding. By means of this approach, we may know what the text basically tells us in terms of the doctrine of the Church. Even before we could deserve in any way his gracious love, God's love granted us the undeserved life of grace. In his initiating love, he loved us first. Most people with some knowledge of catechism understand this meaning of the text, though it may not be understandable to a non-Christian or a poorly educated one.

A formative reading of the same text may also yield formative-inspirational insight. In that case the reader dwells on the text for inspiration and practical guidance of his personal spiritual life. He may be struck by the message that he is submerged in the all encompassing love of the Divine, a love that holds him from eternity. He may sense this love of God for him deeply. From his life experience images and feelings may emerge. For example, he may feel like a little fish in the infinite ocean of love that was there before him and will exist after him. He feels carried by this overflow of divine love without any effort or merit on his part. The inner practice of loving trust and surrender is rekindled and deepened.

This is one of many personally inspirational meanings that could arise from our scripture reading. This personal formative understanding does not contradict the doctrinal one; rather it makes an inspiring practical application to one's personal spiritual life of a text understood already doctrinally and possibly exegetically.

Doctrine and Formative Scripture Reading

Church doctrine protects meditative reading against deviations from the fundamental truths proclaimed by the Church. Most Catholic editions of Holy Scripture contain the necessary footnotes and references to safeguard us against false or purely subjectivistic interpretations. We may also find commentaries on the text of scripture, approved of by the Church, that provide us with an extended service in this regard. It may be helpful to read such commentaries carefully or to follow a course which introduces us into the scriptures. Ideally we should assign another time to this informative reading than the time we have set aside for meditative reading.

The Church is the guardian of the treasures of truth in Holy Scripture; it fixes for us the boundaries of what safely can be believed. If we search for formative meanings of scripture outside these boundaries, we are literally "out of bounds," outside the faith as defined by the Church. The Christian reader respects deeply and is grateful for this outlining of the boundaries. He realizes that the text of scripture contains within these limits set by the Church an inexhaustible reservoir of potential formative directives the Spirit may disclose to individual readers.

Engaged in formative reading, my focus is on a personal penetration of the doctrinally understood text so that it might reveal my life direction in Christ. We can compare the relation between the doctrinal and the formative approach to scripture with drilling for an oil well. One of the most important aspects of drilling is the exact locating by geologists of the place where oil may be found. This locating is done before work on the well begins. Then the spiral drilling starts, going deeper and deeper into the earth, until the hidden treasure of oil gushes forth.

Doctrinal definition outlines the exact location in the sense that this text can basically have only this fundamental meaning. This established significance of the text can then be applied in countless practical and inspirational ways to the spiritual formation of the reader. Meditative reading is a dwelling on the text, drilling and spiraling, so to speak, until the treasure of life transforming meanings springs up. The doctrinal approach to scripture aims thus at an exact locating of its fundamental meaning, a fixing of the boundaries of what safely can be believed, a determining of the extent of possible formative meanings, a distinct outlining of the fundamental truth to which the scripture text is pointing. The Magisterium defines or circumscribes the limits within which what is revealed in scripture can be safely and securely experienced, lived, elaborated and applied.

Scripture Note Book

One of the exercises that might be helpful when engaged in formative reading is that of keeping a scripture note book. We may write down texts that touch our life, that inspire us and deepen the awareness of our life direction. We may add our own spontaneous reflections and prayers if we feel comfortable in doing so.

Writing as a mode of self expression tends to clarify and deepen the scripture experience we try to give form to, no matter how awkwardly. Rereading such scripture notes may reawaken in us reverberations of the original illumination we received when we were engaged in formative reading. In the long run these personal notes provide a kind of log-book or our scripture reading journey. A log-book tells us what the journey was like, how the traveller responded to the challenges along the road, what problems emerged and how he solved them. Indirectly it tells us a lot about the traveller himself and about the direction his life took in its interaction with the perils and pleasures he had to face. The note book we keep on our scriptural reading journey may do the same for us; in retrospect we may gain new insight in the direction God is giving to our lives through the scriptures. Such a note book can only facilitate our formative reading if we use it without agitation or compulsion in solitude and silence of heart.

Formative Scripture Reading As Divine Gift

The asceticism of formative scripture reading offers a path to God's presence. Our experience of his presence in the scriptures may be deepened by a divine gift and gain a quality it could never obtain by self discipline alone. At times his presence in a scripture text may convey an inner peace that passes understanding, a peace the world cannot give. Yet, any effective reading of scripture is a gift even if it would not entail a more vivid experience of his presence as just described.

Because it is a gift, we may ask God to grant it to us. Our very beseeching will remind us that formative reading is his gift, not our doing. This reminder is important. For we may forget our dependence on the Spirit. The Spirit complements and transforms our human attempts to find and unfold our life form in Christ through reading of the scriptures. God wants us to do what is humanly possible to increasingly disclose and live our life form hidden in Christ while remaining docilely open to him. Our efforts show our good will in removing obstacles to his grace; our docility shows our increasing readiness for his gift of enlightened scripture reading when it comes to us in his own good time.

The human attempt to read scripture with docility

and equanimity is a sign of our promise to cooperate with his grace of formative reading once it touches our lives. The human attempt is necessary yet it may tempt us to forget that its outcome is only provisional, a shadow of what is to come, that is, the divine enlightenment of our soul that is a pure gift of the Spirit communicated to us in and through the scripture text.

Personal Scripture Reading and Reading by Others

Formative reading is an art which can be developed by thoughtfully accompanying our own reading with the reading practice of a fellow Christian who seems more proficient and who has perhaps received the charism to put into words clearly and movingly his formative experience. The purpose of this participation is by no means to keep the disciple bound to the experience of such a master. The disciple becomes aware how the latter was able to link the scripture text to our life and destiny. Because the master's experiences may be relevant to the life of many Christians, the inner life of the disciple may often vibrate with the experience of the master.

Nevertheless, it is crucial for his own emergence that the disciple sooner or later try in some measure to advance on his own, moved by his own grace, that he try to associate the text and, if possible, the perception of the master with his own life experience.

This book of formative reflection on a passage of St. John has been written with the same purpose in mind.

The author hopes that the reader, moved by his formative reading of these simple reflections, may have found his own way to the text and has met the Holy Spirit as no one else can meet him.